Observed and Projected Ecological Response to Climate Change in the Rocky Mountains and Upper Columbia Basin

A Synthesis of Current Scientific Literature

Natural Resource Report NPS/ROMN/NRR—2010/220

Isabel W. Ashton
National Park Service
Rocky Mountain Inventory & Monitoring Network
1201 Oakridge Dr, Suite 200
Fort Collins, CO 80525
isabel_ashton@nps.gov

with contributions from:
Stacey Ostermann-Kelm
Tom Rodhouse
Kathy Tonnessen
Ellen Porter
Dave McWethy

June 2010

U.S. Department of the Interior
National Park Service
Natural Resource Program Center
Fort Collins, Colorado

The National Park Service, Natural Resource Program Center publishes a range of reports that address natural resource topics of interest and applicability to a broad audience in the National Park Service and others in natural resource management, including scientists, conservation and environmental constituencies, and the public.

The Natural Resource Report Series is used to disseminate high-priority, current natural resource management information with managerial application. The series targets a general, diverse audience, and may contain NPS policy considerations or address sensitive issues of management applicability.

All manuscripts in the series receive the appropriate level of peer review to ensure that the information is scientifically credible, technically accurate, appropriately written for the intended audience, and designed and published in a professional manner.

This report received formal peer review by subject-matter experts who were not directly involved in the collection, analysis, or reporting of the data, and whose background and expertise put them on par technically and scientifically with the authors of the information.

Views, statements, findings, conclusions, recommendations, and data in this report do not necessarily reflect views and policies of the National Park Service, U.S. Department of the Interior. Mention of trade names or commercial products does not constitute endorsement or recommendation for use by the U.S. Government.

This report is available from Rocky Mountain Inventory and Monitoring Network (http://science.nature.nps.gov/im/units/romn/index.cfm) and the Natural Resource Publications Management Web site (http://www.nature.nps.gov/publications/NRPM) on the Internet.

Please cite this publication as:

Ashton, I. W. 2010. Observed and projected ecological response to climate change in the Rocky Mountains and Upper Columbia Basin: A synthesis of current scientific literature. Natural Resource Report NPS/ROMN/NRR—2010/220. National Park Service, Fort Collins, Colorado.

NPS 960/104295, June 2010

Contents

Figures

Tables

Climate change is having significant effects on organisms and ecosystems worldwide, but changes in the western United States have been particularly rapid over the last 30 years. Resource managers in the West are being asked to manage for ecological responses to climate, but they have limited access to regional or local information on the observed and projected effects of climate change. In this report we synthesize information on the observed and projected responses of selected ecosystem properties and processes, organisms, and communities within the Rocky Mountains and Upper Columbia Basin (ROCO). As defined by climate and geopolitical boundaries, this region encompasses the Greater Yellowstone Area, the Crown of the Continent ecosystem, the Colorado Front Range, the Upper Columbia Basin, and 12 high-elevation units of the National Park System, and most of the US portion of the Great Northern Landscape Cooperative.

Our goals are to: (1) highlight common themes in response to climate change so that resource managers can better identify system vulnerabilities, determine resource program needs, and develop conservation targets, and (2) inform the development of the monitoring systems needed to assess climate change impacts and possible management actions.

We focus on physical and ecological properties and processes, and resources (communities and species) that are relevant to land managers in the ROCO region, including

- air quality;

- ecological processes and properties, including biodiversity and productivity; phenology, connectivity, wildland fire, insect infestations, plant and wildlife disease, and invasion dynamics;

- communities of interest, including alpine and tree line, forests and woodlands, five-needle pines, aspen, sagebrush and grasslands, aquatic systems and wetlands;

- animal species, including grizzly bears, fish, amphibians, invertebrates, birds, pika, and ungulates.

We found that some ecosystem properties, processes, and resources are being affected by warming temperatures and changes in precipitation patterns; this is supported by published evidence of observed responses to climate change within the last century and well-developed hypotheses and models that project a continued response during the next decade. The magnitude and direction of response varies, but these sensitive ecosystem properties, processes, and resources may provide strong indicators of climate change. Climate change indicators for the ROCO region include freshwater resources such as glaciers, wetlands, and fishes; wildlife and plant disease; wildland fire; insect infestations; alpine vegetation; phenology; butterflies; elk; and birds.

For other ecosystem properties, processes, and resources, evidence of climate change has not been found and in many cases other stressors are likely to drive changes over the next century. For instance, grasslands and sagebrush are extremely vulnerable to changes in fire regimes and biological invasions. In other cases, we lack published evidence that links recent trends to climate change, but well-developed hypotheses suggest that the resource may be vulnerable in the future. For example, bats and mountain ungulates are expected to be sensitive to climate change.

As temperatures and precipitation patterns change over the coming decades, a better understanding of how climate change affects resources will become critical to effective mitigation and management. Climate change will interact with multiple stressors, such as land-use change, atmospheric pollution, and invasive species, many of which are more proximate than climate change, making it difficult to predict changes. The only certainty is that ecosystem properties, processes, and resources will continue to change over the next century. Species will be lost, others will be gained, and disturbances will increase and alter the structure and function of ecosystems. Future management, monitoring, and research efforts will need to embrace these changing conditions.

Acknowledgments

We would like to acknowledge all the participants of the 2009 National Park Service (NPS) Rocky Mountain Inventory & Monitoring Technical Committee Meeting. An steering committee including Judy Visty (NPS), Kathy Tonnessen (NPS), Lisa Garrett (NPS), Tom Rodhouse (NPS), Tom Olliff (NPS), David McWethy (Montana State University), Stacey Ostermann-Kelm (NPS), Bruce Bingham (NPS), and Penny Latham (NPS) provided useful comments throughout the process. An inter-agency committee organized through the Great Northern Landscape Cooperative also provided guidance and advice throughout the writing and development process. This committee included: Yvette Converse (FWS), Mike Britten (NPS), Tom Olliff (NPS), Molly Cross (Wildlife Conservation Society), Steve Gray (WY state climatologist), Beth Hahn (USFS), Virginia Kelly (Greater Yellowstone Coordinating Committee), Tim Mayer (FWS), Jim Morrison (USFS), Stacey Ostermann-Kelm (NPS), Greg Pederson (USGS), David Wood (BLM), Andrea Ray (NOAA), and Lou Pitelka (NEON).

Funding was provided by the Greater Yellowstone Coordinating Committee and the NPS Inventory & Monitoring Program. Conceptual models were developed by Stacey Ostermann-Kelm (NPS), Dave McWethy (Montana State University), Tom Rodhouse (NPS), and Isabel Ashton (NPS), and designed by Robert Bennetts (NPS). Maps were created by Meghan Lonneker (NPS). We acknowledge and thank Mary Ann Franke (NPS), Emily Yost (Utah State Univeristy), and Tami Blackford (NPS) for assistance with formatting and editing this document.

The content of the manuscript was greatly improved by comments from Julio Betancourt (USGS), John Gross (NPS), Mike Britten (NPS), Stacey Ostermann-Kelm (NPS), Frank Rahel (University of Wyoming), Geneva Chong (USGS), George Malanson (University of Iowa), Dan Binkley (Colorado State University), Anne Schrag (World Wildlife Fund), Tom Rodhouse (NPS), Tom Olliff (NPS), David Cooper (Colorado State University), David Wood (BLM), Rick Sodja (USGS), Virginia Kelly (Greater Yellowstone Coordinating Committee), Ellen Porter (NPS), Clint Mulfield (USGS), Jason Sibold (Colorado State University), Kathy Tonnessen (NPS), Molly Cross (Wildlife Conservation Society), Beth Hahn (USFS), Lou Pitelka (NEON), and Penny Latham (NPS).

Chapter 1: Introduction

Climate change is having significant effects on organisms and ecosystems worldwide. Changes in the western United States have been particularly noticeable in the last century, with increases averaging 0.5–2°C (0.9–3.6°F) in mean annual temperatures, depending on elevation (Diaz and Eischeid 2007, Pederson et al. 2010). Warmer winters and springs have resulted in more precipitation falling as rain instead of snow, reduced snowpack, earlier snowmelt, earlier streamflow from snowmelt, an 8 to 10 day advance in the onset of spring on average across the West, more frequent large fires, and possibly an increase in insect outbreaks and plant mortality (Cayan et al. 2001, Stewart et al. 2005, Breshears et al. 2005, Mote et al. 2005, Knowles et al. 2006, Westerling et al. 2006, Raffa et al. 2008, Pederson et al. 2010). The preponderance of evidence suggests that the magnitude of these changes has been influenced by human activity. Barnett et al. (2008) used nested climate and hydrological models to attribute most of these changes in the West to greenhouse gas emissions and

their impact on global and regional climate. Another modeling study suggests that these changes are caused by a blend of anthropogenic forcing and Pacific and Atlantic decadal variability (Wang et al. 2008).

Resource managers in the West are being asked to manage for ecological responses to climate trends, but they have limited access to regional or local information about the observed and projected effects of climate change (Lawler et al. 2010). This report and a companion report focused on climate (McWethy et al. in press) are meant to fill this gap by providing land managers with a summary of past, current, and projected climate changes and a description of some of the ecological consequences of climate change in the Rocky Mountains and Upper Columbia Basin. Here, we focus on known and predicted ecological effects and the uncertainties associated with these predictions. Our coverage of topics is not comprehensive; we chose to focus on ecosystem properties and processes, species, and communities

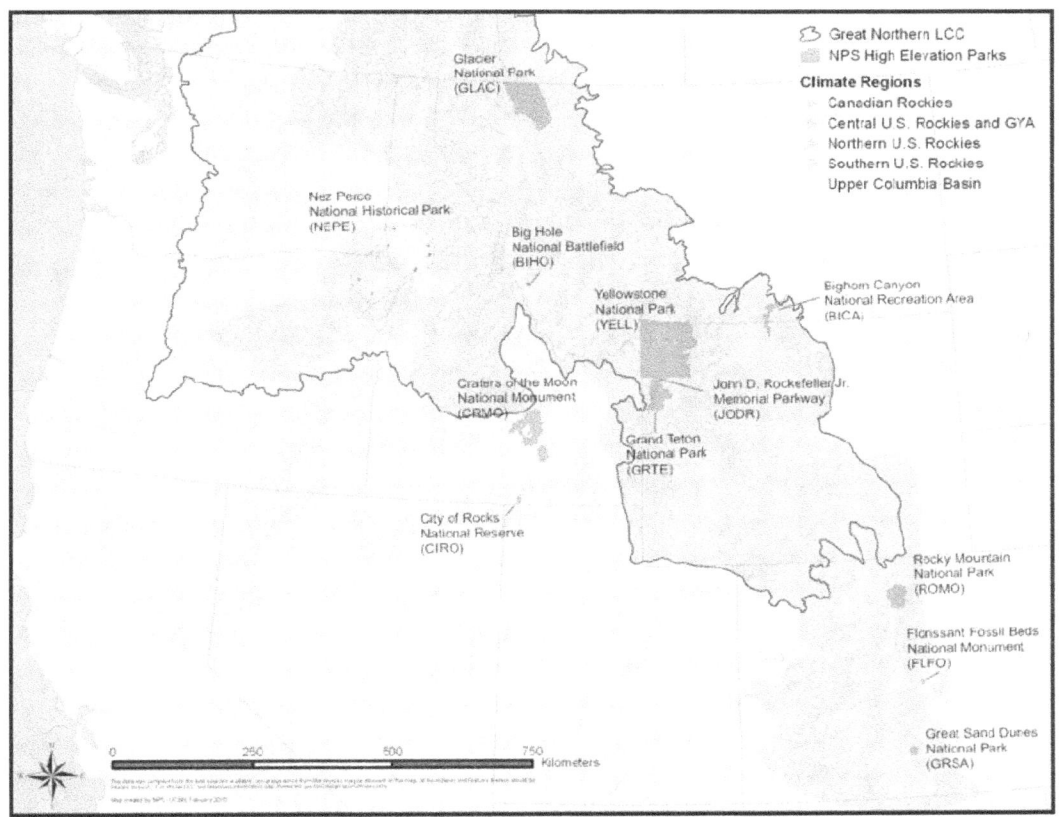

Figure 1. The geographic scope of this synthesis includes the Upper Columbia Basin and Northern, Central, and Southern Rockies. These regions encompass most of the Great Northern Landscape Conservation Cooperative, the Greater Yellowstone Area and 12 high-elevation units of the National Park System.

that are especially relevant to land managers in the area as indicated by the NPS Inventory & Monitoring Vital Signs Plans for the Greater Yellowstone, Upper Columbia Basin, and Rocky Mountain networks (Jean et al. 2005, Britten et al. 2007, Garrett et al. 2007) and discussions with an interagency panel of advisors.

Defined by geopolitical and climate boundaries, the geographic scope of this report includes four regions: the northern US Rockies, the central US Rockies and Greater Yellowstone Area, and the southern US Rockies (fig.1). We refer to this area as the Rocky Mountain and Upper Columbia Basin region (ROCO). It includes most of the US portion of the Great Northern Landscape Cooperative and 12 high-elevation units of the National Park System that are at particular risk with climate change. The area overlaps the National Ecological Observatory Network's (NEON) Northern Rockies Domain and includes portions of the

Southern Rockies–Colorado Plateau and the Great Basin domains. The area also includes numerous units within the USDA Forest Service's Northern, Rocky Mountain, and Intermountain regions.

We have two goals for this ecological synthesis: (1) to highlight common themes in response to climate change so that resource managers can better identify system vulnerabilities, determine resource program needs and develop conservation targets, and (2) to inform the development of the monitoring systems needed to assess climate change impacts and possible management actions. Options for managing ecosystems in the face of global environmental change are not discussed in this document and we recommend turning to some of the exceptional resources for guidance (e.g., Millar et al. 2007, Williams et al. 2007, Baron et al. 2008a, Baron et al. 2008b, Galatowitsch et al. 2009, Joyce et al. 2009, Mawdsley et al. 2009).

2.1 Climate

A review of the currently available information on paleoecological, historical, and projected climate trends in the ROCO region has been produced as a companion document by McWethy and colleagues (in press). Here, we briefly describe the regional climate and observed and projected trends in climate to provide context for possible ecological responses.

At present, the climate becomes warmer and drier when moving south from the northern Rockies and Upper Columbia Basin to the southern Rockies (fig. 2). Climate in the ROCO region is influenced by the Rocky Mountains, which present a barrier to the westerly flow of the atmosphere carrying moisture from the Pacific Ocean (fig. 1). On the east side of the Rockies, winter precipitation is generated from polar continental air flows and warmer maritime air from the Gulf of Mexico colliding with the mountains. In the summer, the northern Rockies may continue to receive moist Pacific air, but the southern and central Rockies receive dry continental air or monsoonal flows from the Gulf of Mexico and Gulf of California (Kittel et al. 2002). Total annual precipitation and January precipitation are greater in the northern Rockies than in the central and southern Rockies (fig.2). January temperatures in the northern Rockies and Upper Columbia Basin tend to be slightly warmer than those of the central Rockies (fig. 2) (Kittel et al. 2002).

2.1.1 Observed trends
Since 1900, temperatures have increased 0.5–2˚C (0.9–3.6˚F) in most areas of the western United States (Pederson et al. 2010, Mote 2003, Ray et al. 2008) but cooling has occurred at some sites (Ray et al. 2008, CIG 2010). The rate of change varies by location and elevation but is typically a 1°C (2°F) increase since the early 20th century (Hamlet et al. 2007). Temperature increases are more pronounced during the cool season (Hamlet and Lettenmaier 2007). In the northern US Rockies, annual rates of increase are roughly 2–3 times that of the global average (Vose et al. 2005, Bonfils et al. 2008, Pederson et al. 2010, Hall and Fagre 2003), a pattern that is evident at northern latitudes and higher elevation sites throughout the West (Diaz and Eischeid 2007, National Assessment 2001). Rises in temperature appear to be accelerating where mean regional spring and summer temperatures for 1987 to 2003 were 0.87˚C (1.57°F) higher than those for 1970 to 1986, and were the warmest since 1895 (Westerling et al. 2006).

Trends in precipitation in the ROCO region are far less clear. Instrumental data from the last century show modest increases for much of the northwestern United States (Mote et al. 1999, Mote 2003, Mote et al. 2005), but no directional trends for parts of the southern Rockies (Ray et al. 2008). Natural variability in precipitation is evident in the instrumental record for all of the climate regions, and long-term drought conditions during the last century impacted large areas within the region. Although 20th century droughts had substantial socioeconomic and ecosystem impacts, there is ample evidence that they were not as severe, in terms of duration and magnitude, as a number of drought events

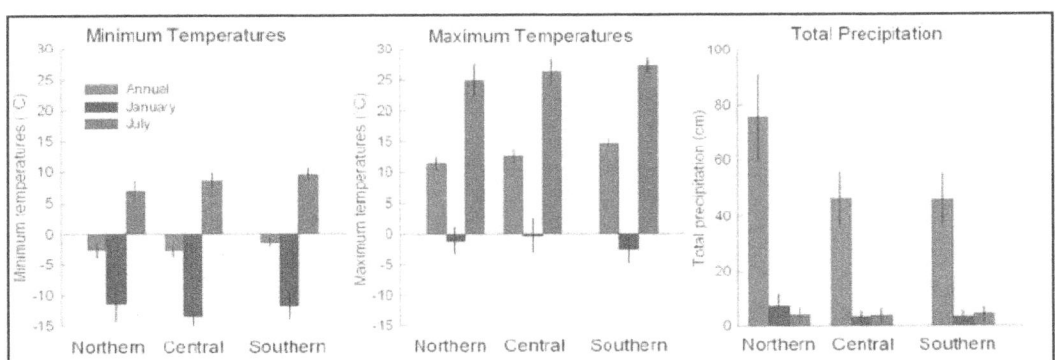

Figure 2. Average minimum temperature, maximum temperature, and total annual precipitation during 1980 to 1997 in the northern Rockies (including the Upper Columbia Basin), the central Rockies, and the southern Rockies. Bars indicate means ±1 interannual standard deviation. Data from Kittel et al. 2002.

that occurred during the last millennium (Cook et al. 2007, 2004; Meko et al. 2007).

2.1.2   Projected trends

Temperatures in the region are generally expected to increase by approximately 1–2°C (2–4˚F) during the next 50 years with natural variation over years to decades. Precipitation is less well understood, but the projection for total annual precipitation suggests that the dominant pattern in North America will be a wetter climate in the northern tier and a drier climate in the southwestern United States. These and other predicted changes for the Rocky Mountains and Upper Columbia Basin are outlined in Table 1.

2.1.3   Summary

Temperatures in the region have generally increased since 1900 and this trend is predicted to continue. It is estimated that temperature will increase by approximately 1–2°C (2–4˚F) in the next 50 years. Precipitation patterns are less clear, but winters are projected to be wetter and summers drier in the future. These climate changes will continue to affect ecological processes, properties, and resources throughout the ROCO region.

2.2   Air quality and deposition

Air pollution is determined by the amount of emissions, atmospheric processes, and weather in a region. Through its effects on emissions, atmospheric and ecological processes, and weather patterns, climate change may have large effects on air quality (Jacob and Winner 2009). The Clean Air Act regulates six major classes of air pollutants: ground-level ozone, particulate matter, carbon monoxide, sulfur dioxide, nitrogen (N) dioxide, and lead (USEPA 2008a). Of these, ozone and particulate matter are of the greatest concern to human health and visibility. Particulate matter includes the very fine dust, soot, smoke, and droplets that are formed from atmospheric reactions. It is produced by dust from roads, aridification, and erosion and when fuels such as coal, wood, or oil are burned. Ground-level ozone is formed when volatile organic compounds react with N oxides in the presence of sunlight. Volatile organic compounds are released from vegetation, fuels, and industrial processes, while N oxides are emitted from any combustion process, including the burning of fuels in cars, power plants, and industrial boilers. In addition to impairing human health, ground-level ozone can cause foliar damage and decreased photosynthesis and growth in plants.

The major components of acid precipitation and deposition are sulfur dioxide, emitted primarily from power plants burning coal,

Table 1. Summary of Projected Climate Changes in the Rocky Mountains and Upper Columbia Basin (based on McWethy et al. in press).

Climate Variable	General Change Expected	Range of Change Expected	General pattern	Confidence
Temperature	Increase	1.5–2.1°C (2.7°–3.4°F)	Increases slightly greater in the summer	High
Precipitation	No change	2–5% increase in winter, 0–4% decrease in summer	Increase in winter, decrease in summer	Moderate for winter; low for summer
Drought	Increase in frequency and severity	Varies with magnitude of temperature and evaporation change	Greatest impact in summer	High
Temperature Extreme Events	Increase of warm events, decrease of cold events	Varies with magnitude of temperature change	Increase in frequency and length of hot events	High
Precipitation Extreme Events	Potential for decreased frequency coupled with increased intensity	Uncertain	Potential for more intense spring and summer floods	Uncertain

and N dioxide, emitted from cars and power plants. Both can cause the acidification of soils, streams, and lakes. Since N is a limiting resource in many communities, N deposition can also cause unnatural fertilization, with cascading effects on ecosystem health (Galloway et al. 2003). Excess N often favors invasive plant species, enabling them to outcompete native species. In Rocky Mountain National Park, N from atmospheric deposition has caused increased nitrate in lakes, increased N in vegetation and soils (Baron et al. 2000a; Baron et al. 2003), and changes in aquatic biota (Baron 2006). Current levels of N deposition in the park are sufficient to alter alpine plant community composition (Bowman et al. 2006). In the Upper Columbia Basin Network, N deposition may be contributing to the invasion of cheatgrass, which is known to be responsive to elevated soil N (Chambers et al. 2007, Lowe et al. 2003, Monaco et al. 2003).

Toxics such as mercury, which is emitted primarily by coal-burning power plants, can accumulate in the environment, posing severe threats to human and wildlife health. The Western Airborne Contaminants Assessment Project found elevated levels of mercury in fish in some western parks. In Rocky Mountain National Park, mercury concentrations in some fish exceeded contaminant health thresholds for some piscivorous mammals (otter and mink) and birds (kingfishers). Concentrations of other airborne toxics, including dieldrin, dacthal, and endosulfan, were also elevated in fish, and some fish showed symptoms of endocrine disruption (e.g., poorly developed testes and intersex male trout) (Landers et al. 2008).

2.2.1 Observed trends
From 1970 to 1997, aggregate criteria air pollutant emissions decreased 31% across the United States while the US population, the number of vehicle miles traveled, and the gross domestic product increased (USEPA 1998). Since 1990, air quality has improved significantly for all major classes of pollutants; the greatest reductions occurred in sulfur dioxide, carbon monoxide, and lead (USEPA 2008b). Reductions in emissions are primarily a result of increased regulation and are independent of climate effects. As with

the rest of the nation, sulfur dioxide emissions from power plants have generally been reduced in the ROCO region, but emissions of N oxides and volatile organic compounds from oil and gas production have increased. Ammonia, which is emitted from agriculture, feedlots, and automobile catalytic converters, also appears to be increasing, but because it is not a regulated air pollutant, emission levels are uncertain. Ground-level ozone has increased in areas with high levels of energy development due to increased traffic, road development, and diesel use.

From 1993 to 2004, deposition and snowpack records for the ROCO region show a marked decrease in sulfate deposition in the northern, central, and southern Rockies (Ingersoll et al. 2008). However, ammonium (from ammonia) and nitrate (from N oxides) concentrations in snow increased during that period in the southern and central Rockies (Ingersoll et al. 2008). Compared to the rest of the United States, N deposition in the Intermountain West is fairly low, but the ecological consequences, particularly in alpine areas, are great (Bowman et al. 2002; Baron et al. 2003, Baron 2006). Alpine ecosystems are poorly suited to assimilating N because of their short growing season, low vegetative cover, low ambient soil nutrients, and high rates of snowmelt flushing (Baron et al. 2000a, Williams and Tonnessen 2000). Nitrogen causes changes in alpine ecosystem structure and function and can contribute to acidification of alpine streams, lakes, and soils (Fenn et al. 2003).

2.2.2 Projected trends
A warmer climate will make it more difficult to meet US air quality standards, particularly for ozone (Field et al. 2007, Karl et al. 2009). Changes in climate affect air quality by changing wind patterns and ventilation rates, precipitation, dry deposition, chemical production and loss rates, natural emissions, and background concentrations (Jacob and Winner 2009). For instance, higher temperatures increase the oxidation of sulfur and N oxides, and precipitation changes will influence the distribution of acids deposited across the landscape (Bernard et al. 2001).

Some of the better understood effects from

a warmer climate include increased ground-level ozone formation and increased particulate matter derived from forest fires. Ozone formation generally increases at higher temperatures due to increased gas-phase reaction rates (Aw and Kleeman 2003). The rate at which volatile organic compounds are produced from natural sources, such as trees, will also increase with increasing temperatures (Guenther 2002). This may be somewhat offset by the inhibitory effect of carbon dioxide (CO_2) on isoprene production (Young et al. 2009), as isoprene is one of the more significant ozone precursors emitted by vegetation. Most models find that even with current emission rates, there will be a widespread increase in ground-level ozone during the summer over the next century (Jacob and Winner 2009). This is consistent with historical data that show a consistent increase in ozone with temperature in polluted areas (Jacob and Winner 2009). In the West, however, decreases in background concentrations of ozone (due to increased water vapor) may offset increases in ozone due to temperature (Jacob and Winner 2009).

There is no consensus among models on the predicted effect of future climate on particulate matter (Jacob and Winner 2009). However, climate change may indirectly affect the concentration of particulate matter in the air by increasing natural sources such as wildfires and global and regional transport of dust (USEPA 2008b), resulting in decreased visibility in downwind areas. This may be particularly relevant in western North America, where 6.7 times more forested area burned from 1987 to 2003 than from 1970 to 1986 (Westerling et al. 2006).

Increased temperatures may exacerbate the effects of N deposition by increasing the rate of N cycling in soils, producing more available N. Increased temperatures are also releasing stored N from rock and ice glaciers. In Rocky Mountain National Park, recent increases in alpine stream nitrate appear to be related to increased melting of glaciers (Baron et al. 2009). Results from a modeling

study by Civerolo and colleagues suggest that N deposition in eastern watersheds during the summer may increase 3–14% as a result of increased precipitation, while dry N deposition is predicted to increase because higher surface temperatures favor gas-phase nitric acid to particulate nitrate (Civerolo et al. 2008). However, other modeling predicts that planned emissions reductions will offset temperature-related increases in N and sulfur deposition in many parts of the country, with some exceptions in the West (Tagaris et al. 2008).

The fate of toxics such as mercury in a changing climate is poorly understood, but it is expected that increased volatilization will transfer mercury between ecosystems via atmospheric transport, re-depositing it in a more mobile and potentially more toxic form (Jacob and Winner 2009). However, if a drier climate results in a loss of wetlands, aquatic systems may have less mercury methylation.

Model-based predictions of air pollution in a changing climate are fraught with uncertainties (Bernard et al. 2001). Emission inventories vary in accuracy and unregulated pollutants like ammonia are poorly accounted for. While national and international emission regulations play a major role in regulating air pollution, they vary in effectiveness. There are additional uncertainties in our understanding of atmospheric chemistry processes, predictions of precipitation changes, and the role of meteorology in air quality (Jacob and Winner 2009).

2.2.3 Summary

Despite uncertainties, air pollution is expected to increase in a warmer climate. Much evidence suggests that the frequency and duration of ground-level ozone events will increase. Remote areas may be most affected by changes in the global background of ground-level ozone and by increases in particulate matter due to increases in fire frequency and drought. Wet and dry deposition of N and sulfur compounds will be sensitive to changing precipitation patterns and mercury deposition may increase.

Climate change has led to fundamental alterations in ecosystem properties and processes. In this section we summarize observed trends and projected responses to climate change for some of those that are likely to be affected: biodiversity, productivity, phenology, connectivity, wildland fire, insect infestations, plant and wildlife disease, and invasion dynamics.

3.1 Biodiversity

The Secretariat for the Convention on Biodiversity (2003) defines biological diversity as including all plants, animals, microorganisms, the ecosystems of which they are part, and the diversity within species, between species, and of ecosystems. Understanding and managing for the response of biodiversity to climate change presents one of the greatest challenges to land and resource managers in the West. The diverse and varied topography in the ROCO region, particularly in the mountains, contributes to high community diversity compared to the eastern United States, although any one community may have relatively few species (Wickham et al. 1995). Diversity is positively correlated with area such that larger patches of habitat contain more species than do smaller patches (MacArthur and Wilson 1967). Habitat fragmentation and loss causes decreases in diversity. Other non-climate stressors threatening diversity include invasive species, disturbance, and pollution. On the global scale, it is believed that biological diversity will decline in response to climate changes (Parmesan and Yohe 2003, SCBD 2003). Below, we describe some of the observed and predicted trends for diversity in the ROCO region.

3.1.1 Observed trends
Historical and paleoecological data suggest that climate can drive alterations in vegetation productivity, diversity, abundance, and composition (e.g., Pederson et al. 2007). These changes in plant diversity and communities are mirrored by concurrent or subsequent changes in animal diversity. Yet there have been few examples of climate-driven extinctions or extirpations of species during the last century; instead the primary drivers have been disease, invasive species, dams and hydrologic alterations, hunting pressure, and land-use change (Tomback and Kendall 2002). One exception is the decline of rare alpine plants in Glacier National Park which is thought to be due to warmer temperatures (Lesica and McCune 2004).

3.1.2 Projected trends
With a 1°C (2°F) increase in average global temperature, the IPCC estimates that up to 30% of all species will be at increased risk of extinction (Field et al. 2007). While such models and estimates include uncertainties, there is little or no evidence that climate change will slow species loss (SCBD 2003). The Secretariat for the Convention on Biodiversity (2003) predicted four impacts on biodiversity as a result of climate change: (1) the climatic range of many species will move poleward or upward in elevation; (2) many species that are already vulnerable, such as rare endemics and threatened and endangered species, are likely to become extinct; (3) changes in the frequency, intensity, extent, and locations of climatically and non-climatically induced disturbances will affect how and at what rate existing ecosystems will be replaced by new plant and animal assemblages; and (4) some ecosystems, such as high mountain ecosystems, arid ecosystems, remnant native grasslands, and ecosystems underlain by permafrost, will be particularly vulnerable to climate change. Diversity will decline where habitats are found in small discrete patches, such as alpine tundra and lakes, and where warming contributes to habitat loss.

3.1.3 Summary
Most evidence suggests that changes in biodiversity will occur, and that they will be spatially and temporally variable. Certain species, such as rare or threatened species, and certain communities, such as alpine wet meadows, are at particular risk of extinction or loss. Rare plants and animals with limited capacity to disperse are particularly vulnerable to loss. The rate of species loss and turnover will vary with the intensity of other stressors such as land use changes, the

spread of invasive species, and changes in disturbance regimes.

3.2 Productivity

In ecological terms, primary productivity refers to the rate of biomass generation by plants and other autotrophs and is often expressed in terms of growth or carbon gain. Experiments and latitudinal patterns suggest that productivity is positively correlated with diversity (Loreau et al. 2001); however, the potential mechanisms behind these patterns, such as increased facilitation, statistical biases, or niche differentiation, continue to be debated (e.g., van Ruijven and Berendse 2005). Patterns of productivity are similar to those of diversity and are driven largely by precipitation, temperature, elevational, and soil gradients; productivity is greatest in warm, wet, and low elevations. Changes in precipitation patterns, fertilization by increased atmospheric CO_2 levels, and changing disturbance regimes make forecasting productivity changes difficult.

3.2.1 Observed trends

In recent decades, warmer temperatures and changing precipitation regimes have increased primary productivity on a global scale and particularly in the Northern Hemisphere (Field et al. 2007). Global daily satellite data indicate that the earlier onset of spring by 10–14 days has contributed to net primary production in the continental United States increasing nearly 10% from 1982 to 1998 (Boisvenue and Running 2006). The most common measure of long-term trends in productivity comes from forest growth. It appears to be slowly accelerating in regions where tree growth has historically been limited by low temperatures and short growing seasons, such as boreal regions and eastern forests, but it is slowing in areas subject to drought or other large-scale disturbances such as fire and insect infestations (Field et al. 2007). Overall, US forest productivity has generally been increasing since the middle of the 20th century (Boisvenue and Running 2006). Where productivity has increased, it is difficult to determine whether climate is the sole cause because of the confounding effects of increased N deposition, increased CO_2 concentrations, and succes-

sional changes.

3.2.2 Projected trends

Although primary productivity is projected to increase moderately due to longer growing seasons and elevated CO_2 concentrations, net ecosystem and biome productivity may decline due to increased disturbance, drought, and changes in community structure. While models project that a modest warming will lead to greater tree growth in the United States (Ryan et al. 2008), there will be spatial and temporal variations depending on other factors that limit productivity at a given site (Ryan et al. 2008). This may result in a pattern of initial gains in productivity followed by declines. The areal extent of drought-limited ecosystems is expected to increase by 11% for each 1°C (2°F) of warming in the continental United States (Bachelet et al. 2001). For widespread species such as lodgepole pine (*Pinus contorta*), a 3°C (5°F) temperature increase would increase growth in the northern part of its range, decrease growth in the middle range, and decimate southern forests (Rehfeldt et al. 2001). Where climate change leads to conversions of vegetation type (e.g., woodland to grassland), this will have strong impacts on productivity (Izaurralde et al. 2005).

3.2.3 Summary

Modest increases in productivity and forest growth are expected in the West with warmer temperatures. However, in areas subject to drought and decreased precipitation, productivity will likely decline.

3.3 Phenology

Phenology is the study of the seasonal timing of events in the annual life cycle of plants and animals in relation to climate. Leaf-out, flowering, senescence, animal migrations, hibernation, and insect emergence are examples of phenological events. The timing of these events is of interest to many birdwatchers, gardeners, and other citizens, and they are critical to many economic activities, such as agriculture. The timing is sensitive to seasonal and interannual variations in temperature and precipitation. Thus phenology is considered the gateway to climatic effects on biota and ecosystems and is vital to the public interest. As a consequence, there are extensive phenological records from around the globe and across many taxa. Most of these records show some evidence of recent changes due to increasing temperatures (Parmesan 2006). At a global scale, they indicate that there has been a mean advance of spring events of ~2.3 days per decade during the last century (Parmesan and Yohe 2003).

3.3.1 Observed trends

Although long-term records of phenology are scarce in the West compared to other regions, here are a few examples.

- From 1957 to 1994, flowering of lilacs (*Syringa vulgaris*) and honeysuckle (*Lonicera tatarica and L. korolkowii*) have shown an advance of 7.5 and 10 days, respectively, in the West. This is most likely due to the 1–3°C (2–5°F) increase in spring temperatures during that period (Cayan et al. 2001).

- In Lake Washington, near Seattle, the timing of phytoplankton blooms advanced 19 days from 1962 to 2002 because warmer spring temperatures have changed the timing of stratification (Winder and Schindler 2004).

- At the Rocky Mountain Biological Laboratory in the southern Rockies, yellow-bellied marmots (*Marmota flaviventris*) emerged from hibernation significantly earlier in 1999 than in 1976 (Inouye et al. 2000).

- Earlier emergence of flowers since 1992 in the southern Rockies has been documented, exposing some plant species to increasing damage from late frosts (Inouye 2008).

Changes in the timing of migration, hydrological events, and fire seasons are discussed in subsequent sections.

3.3.2 Projected trends

With continued warming, we should expect to see a continued advance of spring in the ROCO region. Compared to 1950 to 1970, streamflow and peak snowmelt are occurring 1–4 weeks earlier (Stewart et al. 2005). Lack of good phenology data make predictions difficult, but changes in the timing of spring will likely affect the timing of reproduction, emergence, and migration of numerous species, which may affect community structure and function. On the other hand, phenological events that are tied to day length, such as the emergence of many plants, are not expected to change.

While evolutionary adaptations to climate change can be rapid, it is generally thought that they are not rapid enough to counter the negative effects that climate change will have on many species (Parmesan 2006). One concern is the development of asynchronies among interacting and dependent species. For instance, there is the potential for increased stress for marmots in the early spring because while marmots are emerging earlier, there has been no change in the emergence of food plants in the area (Inouye et al. 2000). Mismatches in the phenology of birds and their prey have been documented in other parts of the United States and the globe and have been linked to population declines (Both et al. 2006, Wormsworth and Mallon 2008).

The key uncertainties in understanding the response of phenology to climate change lie in the rate at which phenological changes occur and how fast species will adapt to new seasonal regimes. Manipulative experiments suggest that other global changes, such as changing CO_2 concentrations and increased nutrient availability, may dampen the phenological response to warming (Cleland et al. 2006). As a result, it will be difficult to predict the magnitude and direction of response for many species. There are also apparent contradictions between individual species and ecosystem level responses (Steltzer and Post 2009). Moreover, it remains unknown how often and how many species interactions will be affected by the development of asynchronous life histories. Finally, the largest changes to date are related to earlier spring onsets; less is known about phenological changes to climatic trends in other seasons.

3.3.3 Summary

Phenological observations provide inexpensive, useful, and sensitive records on the ecological consequences of climate change.

Globally, there has been a trend for species to advance timing of many life-history events in concert with warming temperatures. In the West, records suggest that warmer spring temperatures have affected first flowering, hibernation, and lake productivity and these changes are expected to continue.

3.4   Connectivity and animal and plant movement

Connectivity is the measure of the extent to which organisms can move between habitat patches (Taylor et al. 1993). Animal and plant movement is critical for migration, dispersal, and acquiring resources throughout a species' home range. Plant migration and dispersal most often occur at a local scale, but plants can migrate long-distances via wind, animal, and water dispersal. The rate of plant migration is driven by generation time because it is dependent on establishment of seedlings and the time it takes for them to reach reproductive maturity (Neilson et al. 2005). Plant migration rate can be roughly estimated by functional group; long-lived, late successional species with large seeds are typically slower to migrate than wind dispersed, small-seeded plants (Neilson et al. 2005).

In the West, some of the best known animal migrations are those of birds, fish, and ungulates. Raptors, waterfowl, and song birds move between breeding grounds in the north and winter grounds in the south along the Pacific and Central Flyways following the spine of the Rocky Mountains (Birdnature 1998). Some species of salmon *(Oncorhynchus* spp.) in the Northwest travel from the Pacific Ocean to the freshwaters of Idaho where they spawn and die, and their young will spend up to two years in freshwater prior to migrating back to the Pacific Ocean (Groot and Margolis 1991). Cutthroat trout (*O. clarki bouvieri)* migrate upstream into high-elevation lakes when barriers are not present (Kruse et al. 1997). Many ungulates in the region, such as elk (*Cervus canadensis*; e.g., Brazda 1953) and mule deer (*Odocoileus hemionus*; e.g., Sawyer et al. 2005), migrate between summer and winter ranges. The pronghorn antelope (*Antilocapra americana*) migrate seasonally throughout the ROCO

region to access winter forage grounds (Hoskinson and Tester 1980, Sawyer et al. 2005). The pronghorn migration between Grand Teton National Park and the Upper Green River Basin follows an invariant path spanning roughly 150 km (Berger et al. 2006) and is believed to be the longest remaining mammal migration in the continental United States (Berger 2004). Bats undertake significant seasonal movements at regional scales between winter hibernacula and summer pup-rearing areas (Cryan et al. 2000, Dobkin et al. 1995). Several bat species migrate from the ROCO area to the Southwest and Mexico (Cryan 2003, Cryan and Brown 2007).

3.4.1   Observed trends

The paleoecological and historical record suggests that plants can migrate in response to changes in climate. Fossil data suggests that trees may have migrated from 100 to 1,000 meters (109–1094 yd) per year in response to climate warming, but these rapid rates are likely driven by just a few long-distance dispersal events (Higgins and Richardson 1999). Over the last century, climate change has driven changes in plant distribution and ranges (Parmesan and Yohe 2003). For instance, alpine plants have shifted upward in elevation in the Alps (Grabherr et al. 1994). In recent times, plant migration has been altered most by humans through accidental and deliberate plant introductions and habitat fragmentation (Pitelka 1997). In some cases, habitat has become so fragmented that dispersal is inhibited, driving plant extirpations (Fahrig 2002).

As with other phenological events, warmer temperatures have driven a trend toward earlier spring migratory arrivals (Parmesan and Yohe 2003). For example, American robins (*Turdus migratorius)* arrived on average 14 days earlier in 1999 than in 1981 in southern Colorado (Inouye et al. 2000), and some 20 species of neotropical migrants arrived in the United States 21 days earlier in 1994 than in 1965 (Price and Root 2005). Migratory routes, while influenced by climate, have been more vulnerable than migratory timing to widespread land-use change and habitat destruction. Berger (2004) estimated that about 75% of the migration routes in the Greater Yellowstone Area for pronghorn, bison and elk have been lost due to human development and agriculture.

Connectivity among habitats is essential to not only allow for migration, but also for linking and maintaining gene flow among disparate populations. Maintaining connectivity has been challenging as human populations and development in the West have increased. Connections between unprotected lowland source populations and mountain populations may be at particular risk. For instance, Hansen and colleagues (2009) showed that American robins and yellow warblers (*Dendroica petechia*) are at risk from human development in the Greater Yellowstone Area because the populations are dependent on breeding in lowland, unprotected areas.

While connectivity is clearly affected by human development, there is less historical evidence from the past century that it has been directly impacted by climate change. Drying of streams and wetlands can reduce connectivity of aquatic habitats (Hauer et al. 1997). Large-scale changes in vegetation patterns seen in the paleoecological record (e.g., Whitlock and Bartlein 1993) changed the structure and linkages of habitat across the West. More recent examples of climate altering habitat connectivity and affecting metapopulation structure may come from pikas *(Ochotona princeps)* and butterflies. Beever et al. (2003) hypothesized that the pattern of pika colony extirpation in the Great Basin is driven by warming and increased isolation. Alpine butterfly (*Parnassius smintheus*) populations have become more isolated from one another in the Canadian Rockies due to losses of subalpine meadow habitat (Roland and Matter 2007). Connectivity may also be affected by climate change through changes in animal behavior. For instance, milder winters allow pronghorns to stay in their customary summer ranges and not migrate (e.g., Jacques et al. 2009), which may result in the population losing its knowledge of migration routes that are necessary in average winters.

3.4.2   Projected trends
While the fossil record suggests that plants can migrate rapidly in response to climate,

it is believed that fragmentation, reduced source population size, and a reduction in animal vectors coupled with an unprecedented rate of climate change will make it unlikely that plant species will migrate fast enough to escape its consequences (Neilson et al. 2005). Variation in the rates and ability of plant species to migrate in the face of change will contribute to the formation of communities that have no current analogues. For instance, rare plants, particularly those with low reproductive rates and large seeds, may migrate more slowly than do annual plants. The effectiveness of plant dispersal and migration will strongly influence not only the structure and function of future terrestrial communities but also feedbacks between climate and the land surface (Higgins and Harte 2006).

Climate change is expected to alter animal movement patterns through its effects on habitat availability and the timing of movement events. One study estimates that predicted climate changes will reduce migrations of neotropical birds 32% and 39% to the Pacific Northwest and Rocky Mountains, respectively (Price and Root 2005). It is expected that the general trend of earlier migrations will continue (Parmesan 2006).

Projected changes in vegetation cover (e.g., Bachelet et al. 2001), loss of snow cover, debris flows, seasonal floods, and declines in surface waters will likely impact the degree of connectivity among habitats. As species' core habitat areas shift across the landscape, shrink in size, or become fragmented, those species' connectivity needs are also likely to be altered (Cross et al. in press). Changes in hydrology might affect the connectedness of aquatic populations and habitats. Extreme weather events may increase the frequency of large-scale disturbances and these in turn may cause increasing fragmentation (Opdam and Wascher 2004).

The more immediate threat and uncertainty of habitat destruction and fragmentation makes it difficult to predict how connectivity will be affected by climate change. We do not have a strong understanding of the connectivity needs of many species under current conditions in most places. Moreover, since the influence of climate change can vary dramatically across a species' range, particularly for birds with long-distance migrations, understanding how climate change will affect migration patterns is difficult (Inkley et al. 2004). In many cases the primary driver of plant dispersal and habitat alterations will be changes in precipitation and disturbance, the direction and magnitude of which is difficult to predict. Many uncertainties remain because different species will be affected by climate change at differing rates and magnitudes, and phenotypic plasticity and changes in behavior in response to changing environmental conditions are highly variable.

3.4.3 Summary
It is predicted that plant and animal movements and connectivity needs will be altered by climate changes. However, responses will likely vary across species and ecosystems. In the paleorecord plant migration has occurred quickly in response to warming. Due to fragmentation and other dispersal barriers, projections estimate that plants will not keep pace with the current rate of climate change. The timing of migration events such as the arrival of birds and movement of ungulates between winter and summer ranges will likely be driven earlier as springs become warmer throughout the region. There remain

large uncertainties in anticipating future patterns of migration due to unpredictable changes in habitats and the development of mismatches between interacting species. Connectivity of animal populations and habitats will decrease due to increased fragmentation driven by climate-induced disturbances or changes in vegetation.

3.5 Wildland fire

Fire is an essential disturbance in the ROCO region (Keane et al. 2002), where it acts to recycle nutrients, regulate succession, maintain diversity, reduce biomass, control insect and disease populations, and regulate interactions between plants and animals (Crutzen and Goldhammer 1993). Variability in climate and fire regimes over the last 20,000 years has strongly influenced forest composition and structure (Whitlock et al. 2002, Whitlock et al. 2003). Although fire plays a key role in determining the structure and function of most habitats in the region, it has less influence in alpine areas, which rarely burn, and in high subalpine forests, which have fire return frequencies of more than 200 years (Keane et al. 2002). Long-term variations in temperature and precipitation patterns have resulted in continuously changing

Figure 3. Annual variations in the area burned by wildland fires in Montana, Idaho, Wyoming, and Colorado, 2002–2009. The large 2002 Hayman fire is evident in Colorado and the 2007 Murphy complex fire in Idaho. Data from NICC 2010.

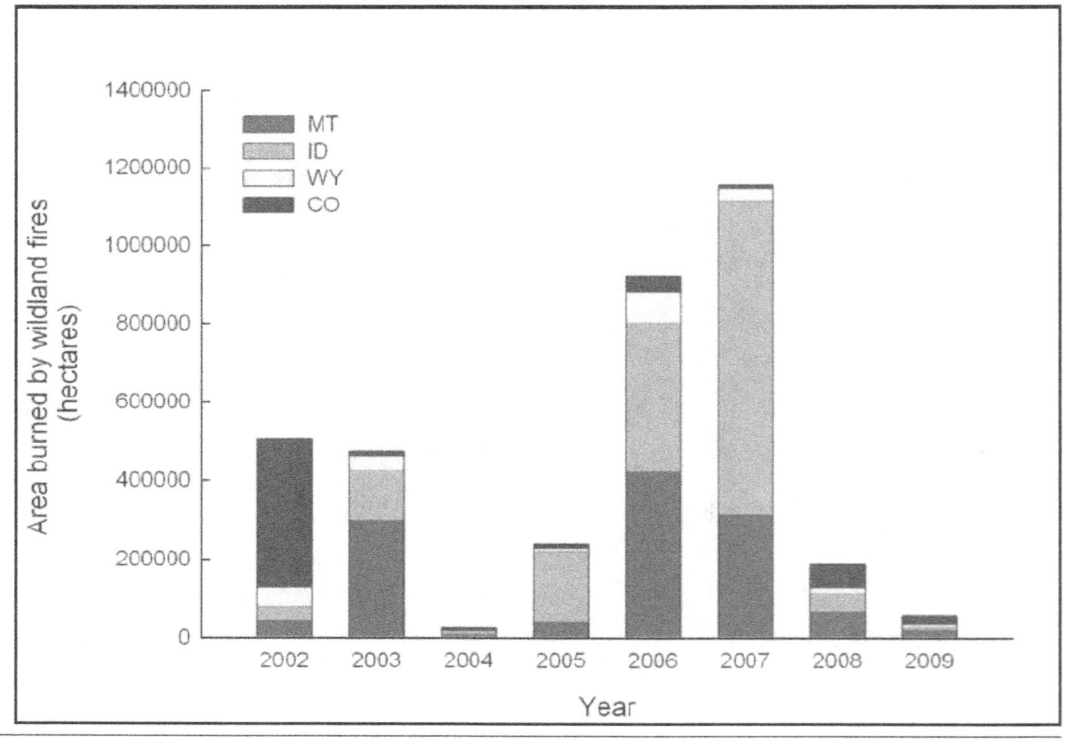

fire regimes (Whitlock et al. 2008). Historical records suggest that an average of 2.4 million hectares (5.9 million acres) burned annually in the northwestern United States prior to 1900, two-thirds of which was sagebrush and grassland vegetation (Keane et al. 2002). Due to fire suppression and changes in land cover, annual fires now typically cover less than half that area (Keane et al. 2002). Large severe fires (>300 acres, 121 ha) account for more than 95% of the area burned in the West in a given year (Peterson and McKenzie 2008). In the ROCO region, the extent of wildland fires varies considerably among years and across states, with the peak season occurring during the summer (Littell et al. 2009) and the largest areas burned typically in Idaho and Montana (fig. 3).

3.5.1 Observed trends

The relative influence of climate on fire behavior varies regionally and by ecosystem type, but generally current-year drought, low winter precipitation, wind conditions, and high summer temperature are positively associated with area burned in the Rockies (Westerling et al. 2006, Littell et al. 2009). In lower-elevation montane forests of the Colorado Front Range, large fires are commonly preceded by wetter than average springs two to four years in advance that presumably increase fine fuel loads (Veblen et al. 2000). Wet antecedent conditions decrease as a contributing factor at higher elevations in the montane zone (Sherriff and Veblen 2008) and are considered unimportant in the subalpine zone where fuels are abundant (Sibold et al. 2006). Other large-scale climate patterns such as the Pacific Decadal Oscillation (PDO; Hessl et al. 2004) and El Niño Southern Oscillation (ENSO; Schoennagel et al. 2005) are also associated with fires, but their strength and signal varies across the ROCO region, with ENSO more influential in the southern Rockies and PDO in the northern US Rockies (Morgan et al. 2008). Additionally, sea surface temperatures in the north Atlantic Ocean (Atlantic Multidecadal Oscillation, AMO) interact with ENSO and PDO to influence the severity and synchrony of drought and fire in the Rockies (Sibold and Veblen 2006; Kitzberger et al. 2007). The complex interactions of the tropical Pacific (ENSO), north Pacific (PDO) and north

Atlantic (AMO) in shaping spatial patterns of drought and fire suggest that projecting the influences of climate change on future patterns of fire is extremely difficult.

The increasing frequency of warm spring and summer temperatures, reduced winter precipitation, and earlier snowmelt in the West during the last 20 years has led to an increase in the frequency of very large wildfires and total acres burned (Westerling et al. 2006). There is insufficient evidence at present to conclude that the increase in the frequency of large fires and total area burned in the northern Rockies since the mid-1980s is outside the range of variation experienced in the last 20,000 years (Whitlock et al. 2008).

Fire dynamics have been altered by climate indirectly through its effects on insect infestations and forest health. By changing the forest environment, bark beetles can influence the probability, extent, and behavior of fire events, but despite the widely held belief that bark beetle outbreaks set the stage for severe wildfires, few scientifically and statistically sound studies have been published on this topic (Negron et al. 2008). That fire promotes beetle infestations is clearer; the fire-caused injury changes conifers' volatile emissions, increasing their susceptibility to bark beetles (Kelsey and Joseph 2003).

3.5.2 Projected trends

Most evidence supports that future climate changes will cause increases in the frequency, intensity, severity, and average annual extent of wildland fires (Field et al. 2007, Ryan et al. 2008). Models project that numerous aspects of fire behavior will change, including longer fire seasons, more days with high fire danger, increased natural ignition frequency and fire severity, more frequent large fires, and more episodes of extreme fire behavior (Brown et al. 2004, Bachelet et al. 2007, Westerling and Bryant 2008). The best evidence, however, is for increases in the average annual area burned (McKenzie et al. 2004, Flannigan et al. 2006, Bachelet et al. 2007). For instance, McKenzie and colleagues (2004) predict that a mean temperature increase of 2.2°C (4.0°F) will increase the annual area burned by wildfire by 1.5 to 5. In another study, it is predicted that the median annual acres burned in the Upper Columbia Basin and northern Rockies would increase from about 0.5 million acres(0.2 million ha) in 1916 to 2006 to 0.8 million acres (0.3 million ha) in the 2020s, 1.1 million acres (0.4 million ha) in the 2040s, and 2.0 million acres (1 million ha) in the 2080s (Littell et al. 2009).

While there is strong evidence that climate change will increase the number of fires, and particularly the area burned each year, uncertainties remain. First, historical patterns of precipitation are linked to fire and synoptic weather features that drive fire growth, such as high pressure ridges and wind patterns, but models differ in their projections for these climate variables. Other factors, such as increases in non-native, annual grass invasions, may alter fire dynamics, making predictions based on climate alone difficult. Finally, and perhaps most importantly, if fires and other stand-replacing disturbances occur more frequently, the resulting landscape pattern may limit the size of future fires and total area burned (Collins et al. 2009).

3.5.3 Summary
Wildland fires have been increasing in frequency and size in the region and are expected to continue to increase with climate change. The increase will be seen most in the total area burned annually and risks will be greatest following dry winters and warm springs.

3.6 Insect infestations

Although abundant in forest ecosystems, insect herbivores typically consume less than 10% of primary productivity. However, the populations of some insect species periodically erupt and consumption increases to well over 50% (Perry 1994). When outbreaks occur, insect herbivores become important disturbance agents in forests, often causing widespread tree mortality on a landscape scale. Insect outbreaks also change forest ecosystem structure and function by regulating certain aspects of primary production, nutrient cycling, ecological succession, and the size, distribution, and abundance of trees (Romme et al. 1986). In 1997, the USDA estimated that insects and pathogens damaged

20 million ha of US forests, which was more than all other disturbance types (e.g., hurricanes, fire, and drought) combined (Dale et al. 2001).

A few of the most common outbreak species in ROCO forests include western spruce budworm (*Choristoneura occidentalis*), Douglas fir tussock moth (*Orgyia pseudotsugata*), and the mountain pine beetle (*Dendroctonus ponderosae*). The western spruce budworm is a widely distributed and destructive forest defoliator favoring Douglas fir (*Pseudotsuga menziesii*), white fir (*Abies concolor*), Engelmann spruce (*Picea engelmannii*), blue spruce (*Picea pungens*), and subalpine fir (*Abies lasiocarpa*) (Leatherman et al. 2009b). Mountain pine beetles attack lodgepole (*Pinus contorta*), ponderosa (*P. ponderosa*), limber (*P. flexilis*), pinyon (*P. edulis*), sugar (*P. lambertiana*), whitebark (*P. albicaulis*), and bristlecone pines (*P. aristata*) (Leatherman et al. 2009a). In some cases and areas, outbreaks are cyclic and fairly predictable. For instance, an outbreak of Douglas fir tussock moths has occurred every 8–10 years in Idaho and British Columbia. In other cases, fire suppression and lack of sub-zero temperatures seem to drive outbreaks and dynamics remain unpredictable.

3.6.1 Observed trends
Although outbreak dynamics differ among species and forests, climate change appears to be driving current insect outbreaks. Western spruce budworm outbreaks were more widespread and lasted longer in the 20th century than in the 19th century primarily because of fire suppression and increasing fir populations (Anderson et al. 1987). However, patterns of spruce budworm outbreaks have been tied to climate in both the East (Gray 2008) and the West (Swetnam and Lynch 1993). There was no clear change in infestation intensity and duration in the southern Rockies during the last three centuries until they became more intense in the 1970s (Swetnam and Lynch 1993). Summer and spring precipitation are positively correlated with increased frequency of outbreaks over regional scales and long time frames, but experimental evidence suggests that drought may promote infestations (Swetnam and Lynch 1993).

Although bark beetle infestations are a force of natural change in forested ecosystems, several current outbreaks occurring simultaneously across western North America are the largest and most severe in recorded history (Bentz 2008). From 2004 to 2008, the area of mountain pine beetle outbreaks increased across Wyoming from 1,000 to 100,000 acres (405–40,469 ha) and the Forest Service has estimated that most of the mature, large-diameter lodgepole forests in southern Wyoming will be dead within 3–5 years (USDA 2008b). In Grand Teton and Yellowstone national parks, mountain pine beetles and the exotic fungal pathogen white pine blister rust (*Cronartium ribicola*) killed more than a half million whitebark pines from 2002 to 2008 (USDA 2008b). The mountain pine beetle has also infested millions of lodgepole and limber pines in Colorado during the past decade and is currently increasing in northern Colorado and the Front Range (USDA 2008a). These outbreaks of bark beetles in the West have coincided with increased temperatures and changes in precipitation patterns, suggesting a response to a changing climate (Shaw et al. 2005). Warming temperatures and the loss of extreme cold days reduce winter overkills of insects, speed up life cycles, modify damage rates, and lead to range expansions, particularly in the north (Logan et al. 2003).

3.6.2   Projected trends

Climate change, and particularly warming, will have a dramatic impact on pest insects, and the recent trends of increasing outbreaks are expected to worsen (Volney and Fleming 2000, Logan et al. 2003). The greatest increase in mountain pine beetle outbreaks is expected to occur at high elevations, where models predict warmer temperatures will increase winter survival (Bentz 2008). At low elevations, however, mountain pine beetle populations may decrease as warmer temperatures disrupt the insects' seasonality (Bentz 2008). Climate change will also alter host susceptibility to infestation. Over the short-term, trees will likely increase in susceptibility to pests due to stress from fires, drought, and high temperatures (Allen et al. 2010); over the long-term, these stresses will cause tree ranges and distributions to change (Bentz 2008). Moreover, climate change

and changes in CO_2 and ozone may alter the conifers' defensive mechanisms and susceptibility to beetles through their effects on the production of plant secondary compounds (Negron et al. 2008).

Insect infestations are damaging millions of acres of western forests and there is clear evidence that damage is increasing. Nonetheless, future predictions of the extent of infestations remain uncertain because our understanding of insect infestations in incomplete. Key uncertainties include the influence of drought and precipitation changes, how altered forest/host composition will alter outbreaks, the biochemical response of trees and evolution of defensive mechanisms, regional differences, and the interactive effects of fire, plant disease, and insect outbreaks.

3.6.3   Summary

Insect outbreaks are already the largest disturbance agent in ROCO forests and they are expected to increase in frequency and severity with warmer temperatures and increasing drought (Logan et al. 2003). Warmer temperatures will allow pests to increase their range northward and upward in elevation.

3.7   Plant and wildlife disease

Plant diseases such as white pine blister rust and sudden oak death (*Phytophthora ramorum*) have had devastating impacts on native forests with cascading effects on wildlife and ecosystems. For instance, blister rust has reduced western white pine (*Pinus monticola*) to less than 5% of its early 20th century population in the interior Pacific Northwest (Harvey et al. 2008). Aspen (*Populus tremuloides*), considered a keystone species in the ROCO region, has suffered substantial declines as a result of fire suppression and a recently-described phenomenon known as sudden aspen decline that may be associated with disease and other pathogens (Worrall et al. 2008).

Emerging wildlife diseases have become a high-priority concern throughout the world because of the potential for their spreading to humans, economic losses associated with livestock morbidity and mortality, and the harmful effects on wildlife populations and ecosystems. The wildlife diseases of greatest recent concern in the ROCO region are (1) chronic wasting disease, which affects ungulate populations; (2) brucellosis, which affects cattle, elk, and bison; West Nile virus, which affects bird populations; and (3) whirling disease, caused by a salmon parasite (*Myxobolus cerebralis*). Numerous other diseases, including rabies, hanta virus, plague, and giardia, threaten wildlife in the region and are of concern because they are zoonotic (shared between humans and animal hosts). Still others, such as white-nose syndrome in bats and avian malaria, are more prevalent elsewhere but present a large potential risk in the ROCO region. In contrast to plant diseases, which are usually slower to appear and spread, wildlife diseases can emerge suddenly and devastate populations. For instance, a recent outbreak of pneumonia in bighorn sheep (*Ovis canadensis)* has been responsible for hundreds of deaths in Nevada and Montana (WSF 2010).

3.7.1 Observed trends

Climate change has altered the dynamics of pathogens and diseases in the past century (Harvell et al. 2002). While a detailed account of climate-induced changes for every disease is beyond the scope of this review, some general trends have emerged.

- Numerous factors along with climate have contributed to disease emergence and increasing transmission risk to humans, including habitat fragmentation, land management practices, road construction, water control systems, and development (Patz et al. 2000).

- Milder winters have made many wildlife and plant species more susceptible to disease because of they have increased the survival of pathogens and the population density of the host organisms (Harvell et al. 2002). For instance, as elk population and herd size has increased in the Greater Yellowstone Area during recent decades, in part due to milder winters (Creel and Creel 2009), so has brucellosis seroprevalence (Cross et al. 2010).

- Warmer water temperatures have increased the virulence of water-borne diseases such as whirling disease (Rahel and Olden 2008). Warmer temperatures may also be contributing to increased mortality of trees in the West (van Mantgem and Stephenson 2007). In another instance, West Nile virus transmissions during the epidemic summers of 2002 to 2004 in the United States were linked to above-average temperatures (Reisen et al. 2009). Laboratory studies are consistent with these trends in which pathogens and parasites can reproduce faster and are more virulent at higher temperatures (Harvell et al. 2002).

- Drought, fire, temperature stress, and extreme weather events are making many host species less resistant to disease and increase the probability of continued spread. For example, mountain pine beetles are a vector for at least three strains of blue-stain fungi (*Grosmannia clavigera)* (e.g., Rice and Langor 2009). Interactions between biotic (mostly fungal) and abiotic stressors (such as drought) may represent the most important effects of climate change on forest diseases (Frankel 2008).

- Climate change is a suspected but not confirmed factor in some disease outbreaks. For instance, over one million bats of six different species have been killed in four years by white-nose syndrome, caused by the fungus *Geomyces destructans* (Blehert et al. 2009). As scientists work to understand the direct cause of mortality and whether climate change is contributing to the spread of the disease, it continues to move westward (NWHC 2010).

In summary, there is ample evidence that climate change has contributed to the increased prevalence and virulence of wildlife and plant disease as well as the increased susceptibility of hosts. The most detectable effect of climate change has been on pathogen range (Harvell et al. 2002). Many vector-borne diseases of wildlife and humans have increased their spread in the last decades with a concurrent spread of the insect vector (Harvell et al. 2002). For example, the spread of avian malaria into higher elevations and northern latitudes is linked to increased minimum temperatures (Patz et al. 2000).

3.7.2 Projected trends

Climate change will likely increase the range, frequency, severity, and impact of plant and wildlife disease (Harvell et al. 2002). The IPCC states with very high confidence that climate change will increase the risk and geographic spread of vector-borne infectious diseases, including Lyme disease and West Nile virus, and changes in precipitation will increase water-borne disease (Field et al. 2007). Diseases will likely move farther north and into higher elevations. For example, the tick that causes Lyme disease, *Ixodes scapularis*, is limited by cold temperature, and models suggest that its range limit could shift north by 200 kilometers (124 mi) by the 2020s and 1,000 kilometers (621 mi) by the 2080s (Ogden et al. 2006). In some cases, climate change may adversely affect the disease rather than the host. For instance, fungal diseases dependent on moist conditions may decrease in a warmer, drier future (Harvell et al. 2002, Frankel 2008).

One of the key uncertainties in predicting the spread of disease is our lack of knowledge about how climate change will affect novel communities that emerge and how dynamics will change as species that have been previously isolated begin to interact. Many wildlife and plants will be exposed to new diseases, but how quickly the dynamics between novel hosts and diseases will evolve remains unknown. Another uncertainty lies with precipitation predictions for the region. Water availability and the combined effects of drought and temperature stress are major factors in forest health, susceptibility to pests and pathogens, and mortality (Allen et al. 2010).

3.7.3 Summary

Climate change will likely continue to increase the prevalence of wildlife and plant diseases. A number of factors are believed to contribute to this, including (1) the direct effect of temperature on the reproduction, spread, and virulence of diseases; (2) novel species interactions; and (3) increased host susceptibility due to temperature, drought, and other stressors. Vector-borne diseases such as West Nile virus and those that are currently limited by low temperatures will increase in elevation and move northward.

Plant communities and wildlife that are faced with multiple stressors are the least likely to resist the emergence of novel diseases.

3.8 Invasion dynamics

Invasive species, defined as those that are alien (non-native) organisms to the ecosystem under consideration and whose introduction causes or is likely to cause economic or environmental harm or harm to human health, are widespread throughout the United States (NISIC 2010). It is estimated that roughly 5% of continental species are alien, and the proportion of plants and freshwater fish that are alien is closer to 10% (Cox 1999). An estimated 25% of the fish species in streams of the western United States are alien (Schade and Bonar 2005). Of the 170 species of native freshwater fish in the western United States, over 100 are listed as threatened or endangered or are candidates for listing, and exotic fish introductions are implicated as a cause in 38% of these listings (Cox 1999).

Approximately 10% of alien species are likely to be problematic invaders (Williamson and Fitter 1996), which results in an estimate of 600 to 700 invasive species in the United States (Cox 1999). The ROCO region is less invaded than areas such as California and Hawaii, but the impacts and extent of invasion can be vast. For instance, the native bunchgrasses of the Upper Columbia Basin and intermountain region have proven particularly vulnerable to over-grazing, allowing extensive areas to become invaded by cheatgrass (*Bromus tectorum*). Millions of acres are at risk of being converted to cheatgrass monocultures with increased risk of frequent wildfire (Chambers et al. 2009). Federal lands and other protected areas have not provided a refuge for native species; 3,756 non-native plant species have become established in 216 US national parks (Allen et al. 2009). Currently, however, high elevations appear to be less vulnerable to invasion, likely as a result of environmental constraints and reduced human development (Pauchard et al. 2009).

The invasive species of greatest management concern in the West fall into three general categories: pests and pathogens, aquatic invaders, and invasive plants. Pests and pathogens, such as whirling disease and the fungus responsible for white pine blister rust, have had devastating impacts on native species. Lake trout (*Salvelinus namaycush),* brook trout *(S. fontinalis)* New Zealand mud snails (*Potamopyrgus antipodarum*), quagga (*Dreissena bugensis),* and zebra mussels (*D. polymorpha*) are some of the most trouble-some aquatic invaders. Brook trout, for instance, have been responsible for the loss of many native trout populations (Peterson et al. 2008). Invasive bullfrogs (*Rana catesbeiana*) have contributed to the decline of native frogs in the ROCO region (Hayes et al. 1986). Plants of the greatest concern are yellow star thistle (*Centaurea solsticialis*), cheatgrass, tamarisk (*Tamarix ramosissima*), leafy spurge (*Euphorbia esula*) and spotted knapweed (*Centaurea maculosa*). These and many other invasive species have contributed to loss of biodiversity, localized extinctions, and changes in ecosystem processes such as fire, hydrologic regimes, and nutrient cycling (e.g., Vitousek et al. 1997, Ehrenfeld 2003, Gurevitch and Padilla 2004).

3.8.1   Observed trends

The spread of invasive species in the West has accelerated in the last decades. For example, from 1986 to 2008, the number of exotic plant species documented in Yellowstone National Park nearly doubled from 105 to 208 (NPS 2008). Non-native annual grasses and forbs have spread throughout grasslands in the West and it is estimated that more than 300 rangeland weed species are present in the United States (DiTamaso 2000). Many species such as quagga and zebra mussels have only recently been sighted in Colorado and on boat trailers in Montana, and are expected to continue to increase in numbers (USGS 2010). While there is a correlation between the spread of invasives and warming temperatures, it is hard to pinpoint climate as the cause because of the many other factors such as lag times, deliberate introductions, and dispersal vectors (Hellmann et al. 2008). Nonetheless, it is suspected that climate is a major driver of the spread of invasive warm-water fishes (Rahel and Olden 2008) and some warm-season grasses (Sage and Kubien 2003).

3.8.2   Projected trends

The spread and impact of invasive species is driven mainly by changes in land use, increasing urbanization, disturbance, and alteration in management practices, but climate change may exacerbate the extent of invasions. Climate change is generally expected to increase the spread of invasive species through direct effects on habitat suitability and the indirect effects of altered nutrient availability and disturbance regimes (Dukes and Mooney 1999). The IPCC has very high confidence that disturbances such as wildfire will continue to increase and this will facilitate invasions (Field et al. 2007). In general terms, invasive species are expected to differ in their response to climate change from native species because they possess traits such as broad climatic tolerances and robust dispersal mechanisms that enable them to better adapt to changing conditions. Hellman and colleagues (2008) identified five consequences of climate change on invasion dynamics: altered invasion pathways, changes in environmental constraints, altered distribution of existing invasive species, altered impacts of invasive species, and a change in management effectiveness. An example of an altered invasion pathway would be an increase in recreational boat traffic as a result of warmer temperatures in previously snow-covered areas resulting in an increase in the spread of nuisance species.

Here are some examples of how climate change is expected to alter invasion dynamics in the ROCO region.

- Stream temperatures are expected to warm with warmer air temperatures and lower flows, increasing the amount of suitable habitat for warm-water fishes by an estimated 31% nationwide (Mohseni et al. 2003).

- Warmer temperatures may increase the impact of invasive species. In the Columbia River, for example, increasing temperatures have caused smallmouth bass (*Micropterus dolomieu)* to consume more native salmon (Petersen and Kitchell 2001), and whirling disease is more virulent in warmer streams (Rahel and Olden 2008).

- Earlier melting of snowpack will alter streamflows, may increase disturbance and flood events, and favor invasive species. It is predicted that such changing conditions may increase rainbow trout (*Oncorhynchus mykiss*) invasions in Colorado (Fausch et al. 2001). However, native species such as cottonwoods could benefit from larger spring flood events that facilitate establishment and recolonization (Scott et al. 1996).

- Bradley and colleagues (2009) examined the current and potential distributions of five problematic plant invaders in the West (cheatgrass, knapweed, yellow star thistle, tamarisk, and leafy spurge) based on the current climatically suitable habitat and maps of future habitat based on an ensemble of global climate models. They found that precipitation was the most important predictor of plant distribution and that warming temperatures alone may have little effect on range expansion. Most species were expected to expand in some areas while contracting in others. For example, they predict that the risk of cheatgrass invasion will increase in Montana, Wyoming, Idaho, and Colorado, but decrease in parts of Nevada and Utah.

There are several uncertainties associated with predicting the ecological response of invasive species to climate change, including how land management, dispersal, and disturbance may obscure climate signals on invasion dynamics. Another challenge in modeling the potential spread of a species is that the physiological limits of many species and their potential to adapt to new conditions is unknown and current habitat suitability may not accurately reflect potential suitability. It is also unclear how climate will alter biotic interactions and current management practices, and how these may alter invasion dynamics. For instance, biocontrol agents may no longer be effective in a changing climate.

3.8.3 Summary

Climate change is likely to increase biological invasions. In the short-term, however, other factors may play a much larger role in the spread and impact of invasive species, including changes in land use and management practices and increasing urbanization and disturbance. Still, models suggest that the following will occur with a warmer climate in the ROCO region:

- Plant and animal species, both native and invasive, will migrate upslope and northward.

- Changes in precipitation will likely drive the expansion and contraction of invasive plants;

- Warmer stream temperatures and a reduction in ice cover will facilitate the spread of aquatic invasives and may increase their impacts.

- Changes in the timing of snowmelt and a subsequent increase in disturbance caused by spring floods may increase the risk of aquatic and riparian invasions.

- Warmer temperatures may change human visitation patterns to natural areas and increase the pathways of spread for many invasives.

Warming temperatures and changing precipitation regimes will likely alter plant and animal communities throughout the ROCO region. Since the timing and magnitude of response to climate change is certain to vary by species, future community assemblages may not have current analogs. Below, we present some concepts that are common across all communities and discuss some of the more specific observed and projected responses to climate change for alpine areas, forests and woodlands, and sagebrush and grassland ecosystems. We also describe how aquatic resources such as glaciers and wetlands respond to climate changes. All of these community types are present within the ROCO region but vary in spatial extent and by locality (fig. 4).

From the paleoecological record it is clear that communities in this region are relatively dynamic and have only recently become established (McWethy et al. in press). To manage terrestrial communities, they must be regarded as a dynamic rather than static assemblage of species. For instance, as many native species expand their range and become established in new communities, distinguishing between native and non-native species will become increasingly difficult.

At a landscape scale, one of the most common ways to understand how terrestrial communities may respond to climate change is through dynamic vegetation models based on current distribution of vegetation and future climate scenarios, and they can also incorporate management strategies, biogeography, and biogeochemistry (e.g., Bachelet et al. 2001). An example of such a model is presented in figure 5. It describes the current distribution of major community types for the United States and two future projections of varying CO_2 emissions and no fire suppression (Lenihan et al. 2008). Overall confidence in model predictions is low because accounting for major drivers of forest structure such as the spread of disease, insect infestations, and land use changes is difficult. How ecosystems will respond to climate is uncertain in specific details, but models are realistic in projecting the kinds and magnitude of changes that we can expect and some general patterns emerge.

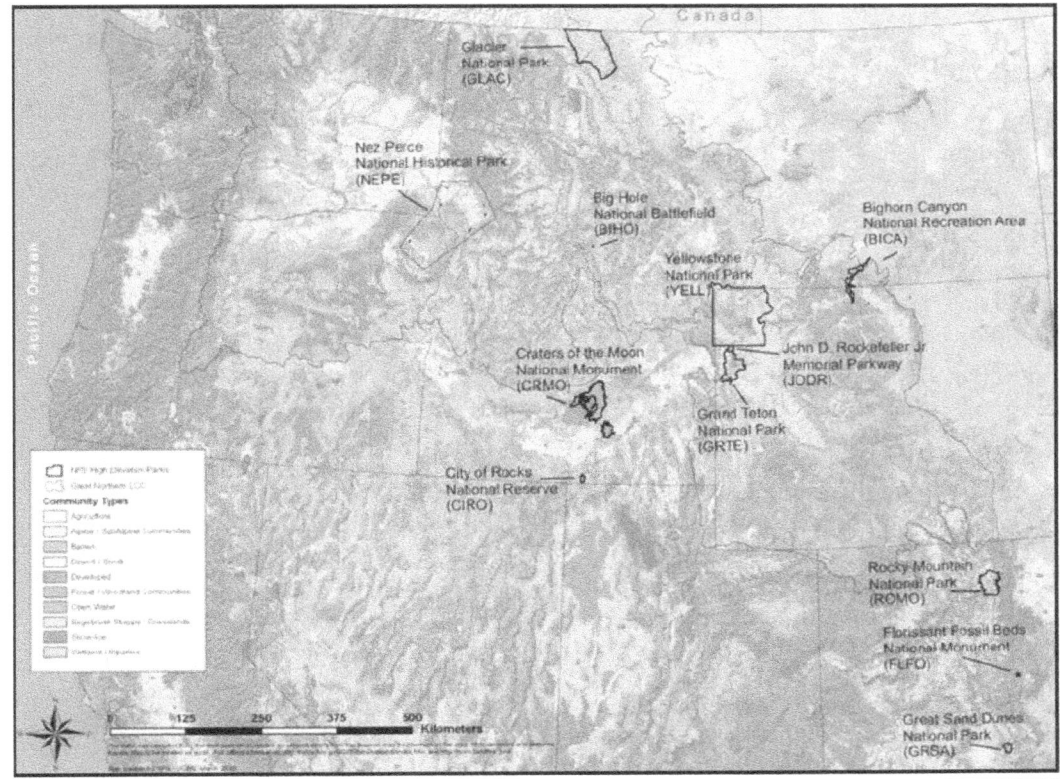

Figure 4. Major community types in the Rocky Mountains and Upper Columbia Basin based on LANDFIRE classification.

Figure 5. Model of simulated vegetation changes assuming unsuppressed fire during 1971 to 2000 (USF-HIST) and two scenarios for 2070 to 2099: a high level of CO$_2$ emissions (USF-A) and a relatively low level (USF-B). Figure from Lenihan et al. 2008.

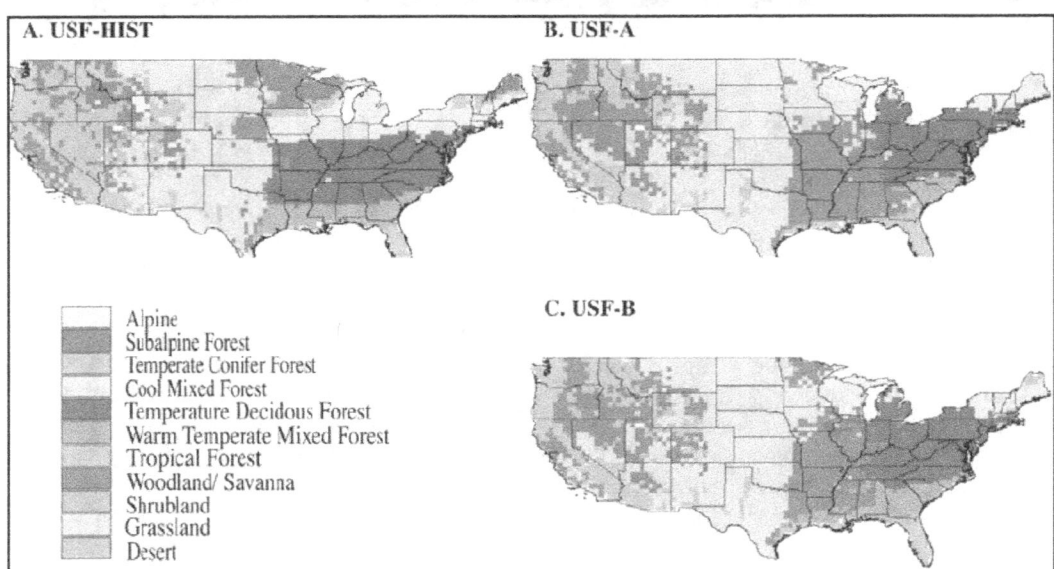

Most simulation models project a widespread reduction in alpine and subalpine forests in the West (fig. 5; Lenihan et al. 2008). The distribution of temperate conifer forests may expand in the northern Rockies and, with limited fire suppression, woodland/savanna vegetation types could replace shrubland areas in the interior West (Bachelet et al. 2001, Lenihan et al. 2008). We discuss some of the drivers and consequences of these changes in the sections below.

4.1 Alpine

The alpine tundra is defined as the vegetation communities that exist above tree line. The alpine/tree line ecotone is found at approximately 3,500 meters (11,483 ft) in southern Colorado, 3,000 m (10,000 ft) in Wyoming, and 2,139 meters (7,017 ft) in northern Montana. The exact location and elevation of tree line varies with climate, topography, snow and debris avalanches, and local competition between tundra and trees (Malanson et al. 2007a), but it is highly temperature dependent and generally concurrent with the 50°F isotherm (where the average July temperature is above 50°, 10°C) (Arno and Hammerly 1984). Alpine and subalpine communities can be found on the highest peaks throughout the region, but the largest areas are found in the Crown of the Continent Ecosystem, the Greater Yellowstone Area, and the Colorado Front Range.

The alpine environment is characterized by high winds, low temperatures, scouring and burial by snow and ice, low nutrient availability, high incident solar radiation, thin atmosphere, and a short growing season (Bowman 2001). The vegetation community is small in stature and dominated by perennial herbaceous species with species composition varying strongly across environmental gradients of water availability, which are driven by snow pack (Walker et al. 2001). The alpine tundra is typically dominated by graminoids and forbs, but nonvascular plants and woody shrubs are also common. Compared to other grassland types, the alpine tundra shows high local diversity (Gough et al. 2000), and the abundance of invasive/exotic species is negligible compared to other ecosystems. The alpine environment serves as refugia for certain species. For example, many Edith's checkerspot butterfly (*Euphydryas editha*) populations have become extinct in the last century, but many fewer have been lost at high elevations (2,400–3,500 m) (Parmesan 1996). Despite its small aerial extent, the alpine environment is considered of high conservation value because of its recreation and aesthetic values. Moreover, it supports numerous animals of management concern, including bighorn sheep, mountain goats (*Oreamnos americanus*), white-tailed ptarmigans (*Lagopus leucura*), and pikas. Most of the water resources in the West are derived from snowmelt, and the quality and quantity of this water is influenced by ecosystem processes in the alpine tundra (Williams and Caine 2001). Because the alpine tundra is globally distributed and particularly sensitive to climate change and atmospheric deposition, it may provide an important indicator for global change (Seastedt et al. 2004).

4.2 Observed trends

At high elevations, warming has positively affected the growth rate of some western tree species, suggesting that as temperatures warm the tree line will continue to move upward (e.g., Salzer et al. 2009). However, compared with the movement indicated by the paleoenvironmental record, direct evidence for upward movement of the tree line in the Rockies due to warming is scarce. In northern Montana, repeat photography shows that the tree line has been stable since the early 20th century and only the density of forest patches at the tree line has increased (Butler et al. 1994, Klasner and Fagre 2002). The tree line has shifted upward in some areas in the Canadian Rockies, but remained stable in others, and changes in fire frequency seem to have had larger effects on forest structure than has climate (Luckman and Kavanagh 2000).

Species that persist in alpine areas have adapted to the extreme environment, but growth and reproduction are strongly limited by environmental conditions and nutrient availability. As a result, warming temperatures and changes in precipitation may strongly influence the persistence of alpine communities. A survey of summit sites in the Swiss Alps showed that vascular plants have been establishing at higher altitudes than recorded earlier (Grabherr et al. 1994). Moreover, the optimum elevation of alpine plants has increased and the shift upward has accelerated during the last century (Walther et al. 2005). Global surveys suggest that one consequence of warming temperatures in the mountains may be an increase in the abundance and distribution of exotic plants (Pauchard et al. 2009). There has been an increase in shrub expansion in the Arctic tundra as a consequence of warming and the altered precipitation of the last century (Sturm et al. 2001), but this has not been documented in the Rockies. There is

some evidence for this from Glacier National Park, where four of seven indicator species have declined in abundance and three have shown no change with the increasing average summer temperatures of the last decade (Lesica and McCune 2004). Warming and changes in precipitation may have large effects on the timing of flowering, which in turn can change pollinator dynamics and plant community structure. Such changes have been seen in montane meadows in the Rockies (Inouye 2008) but have not been documented in the tundra.

4.2.1 Projected trends

Models show that increased temperatures will decrease the abundance and distribution of subalpine trees such as Engelmann spruce in the Greater Yellowstone Area because of the limited extent of alpine area for these species to move into, but predictions are difficult because these trees are sensitive to concurrent changes in precipitation, insect outbreaks, and fire regimes (Schrag et al. 2008). Evidence from recent and paleoecological studies suggest that tree line response to warming varies substantially with the availability of precipitation (Graumlich et al. 2005), adding greater complexity to predictions. In summary, the tree line may shift upward and encroach on alpine tundra in the Rockies as temperatures continue to rise, but it may not be a clear and dramatic change due to variations in local geomorphology, plant response, and human disturbance (fig. 6; Malanson et al. 2007b).

Warming experiments at numerous tundra sites, including one in the Rockies, suggest that a temperature increase of 1–2°C (2–4°F) can increase the height and cover of deciduous shrubs and graminoids, decrease cover of mosses and lichens, and decrease species diversity and evenness (Walker et al. 2006). For instance, warming led to an increase in shrubs and a decrease in forbs in a subalpine meadow in the southern Rockies (Harte and Shaw 1995). Evidence from such experiments and historical data suggest that warming will likely cause changes in alpine community structure and communities with no current or past analogs may develop. Snow is the most important factor driving the current structure of vegetation within the

Figure 6. Conceptual diagram of alpine/subalpine response to climate change.

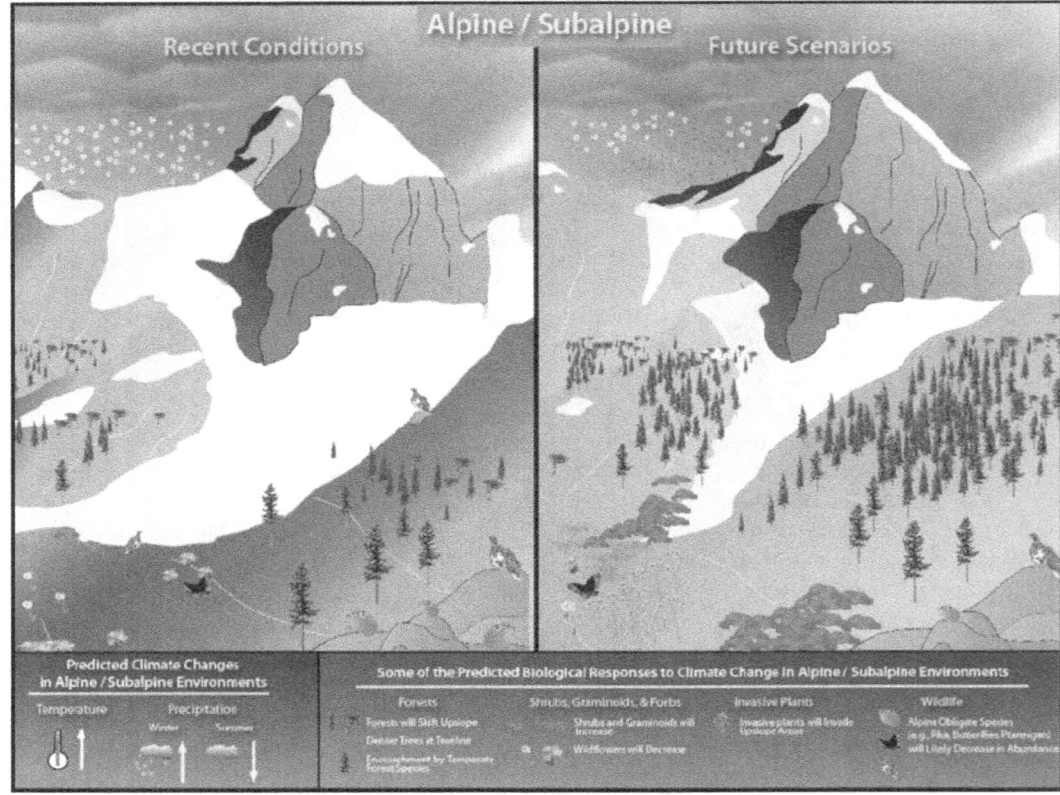

alpine environment, and experiments have revealed that increases in snow depth and duration may enhance the growth of woody species and favor some herbaceous species over others (Walker et al. 2006). The direction of precipitation changes in the alpine and the vegetation response is one of the key uncertainties in describing the alpine response to climate change. Invariably, long-term changes in snowfall and wind deposition of snow will result in changes in the area of wet meadows, fell-field, and dry meadow communities.

The alpine environment is also threatened by other global changes, including the increasing deposition of atmospheric N, ultraviolet radiation, dust storms, insect outbreaks, and fire regimes that may slow the upward migration of the tree line. Perhaps the greatest threat is from N deposition, which has increased in the Rocky Mountains in recent decades due to the growth of metropolitan areas and agriculture (Fenn et al. 2003). Alpine regions in the Rocky Mountains have a low capacity to sequester excess N because of short growing seasons, shallow soils, and steep slopes that encourage rapid run-off

(Fenn et al. 2003). There is evidence that N deposition has altered alpine lake chemistry and biota (Baron et al. 1994) and that it can alter the structure of alpine communities (Bowman 2000). The deposition of dust from storms originating in the arid Colorado Plateau has increased in the southern Rockies (Neff et al. 2008). The dust covers the snow, which changes the albedo and accelerates the timing of snowmelt, which in turn alters alpine phenology and community dynamics (Steltzer et al. 2009). Dust events are also significant inputs of phosphorus and, as with N deposition, have the potential to alter water chemistry and alpine community structure. These multiple stressors on alpine systems add to the difficulty and uncertainty in anticipating how they will respond to climate change.

4.2.2 Summary
The alpine environment is highly sensitive to climate change (fig. 6). From the limited research and monitoring efforts in the Rockies relating to tundra and climate change, it is known that changes will be hard to predict due to local variability and the large influence of precipitation and other global envi-

ronmental changes. Still, evidence suggests that we should expect the following changes with a warmer climate in the Rockies:

- The tree line may increase in elevation in some areas but the response will be complex and dependent on precipitation regimes, fire, and insect outbreaks.

- Subalpine tree species may decline in abundance.

- The density of forests at tree line ecotones may increase.

- Tundra may decrease in areal extent.

- Plant species may migrate upslope.

- Invasive/exotic species may increase in abundance in alpine areas.

- Shrubs and graminoids may increase in abundance while mosses, lichens and some forbs decrease.

- Community composition may be altered with consequences for species that utilize alpine plants, such as pika, mountain goats, and ptarmigans.

- Changes in the alpine tundra will likely be driven by other global changes such as N deposition and dust events.

4.3   Forests and woodlands

Forests and woodlands cover approximately one-third of the United States. Western forests are predominantly coniferous (78%) and in public ownership (57%) (Smith et al. 2001). Of the four states in the ROCO region, Wyoming is the least forested (11 million acres, 4 million ha) while Colorado, Montana, and Idaho each contain roughly twice as much forested acreage (Smith et al. 2001). The dominant forest cover types vary with moisture availability and elevation. At mid-elevations, ponderosa pine, Douglas fir, lodgepole pine, and aspen predominate, while at high elevations, forests are typically comprised of subalpine fir, Engelmann spruce, western white pine, and western larch (*Larix occidentalis*) (Smith et al. 2001). Three-quarters of US lodgepole forests are

found in this region and they are usually dense, pure stands (Smith et al. 2001).

Forests provide valuable wildlife habitat, watershed protection, carbon storage, numerous recreational opportunities, essential gas exchange with the atmosphere, and timber. Over the last century, forest composition has been influenced by management activities, introduced species, forest succession, and natural disturbances such as fire, drought, and insect outbreaks. Fire suppression has been routine in the region since 1900 and, together with planting, has played a major role in determining the current composition of western forests (Keane et al. 2002). Insect outbreaks affect 20 million hectares (949 million acres) of US forest annually, approximately 44 times more area than is affected by fire (Dale et al. 2001). Below we describe some of the observed and projected trends in ROCO forests in response to climate change, then focus on aspen and five-needle pines, two forest types that are of particular management concern.

4.3.1   Observed trends

After the last glaciations ended, warm conditions allowed trees and shrubs to move northward and upslope in many areas (McWethy et al. in press). This suggests that forest composition and tree distribution can respond to climate alterations, but the rate at which these changes will occur in the future remains unclear. There is only limited evidence since 1900 that climate has directly caused compositional changes in forests, but this may be due to lag times. Trees are long-lived organisms and many other factors, such as land management and fire, may have acted to obscure the climate signal. Whatever the cause, forests have changed in composition over the last 100 years. For example, in the Kootenai and Idaho Panhandle National Forests, Douglas fir and other shade tolerant species such as Engelmann spruce have become more abundant as the forest canopy increases while species such as ponderosa pine and western larch have declined (Morrison in prep). An outbreak of white pine blister rust has eliminated an estimated 90% of the western white pine and whitebark pine in the Northern Rockies (Neuenschwander et al. 1999, Kendall and Keane 2001, Harvey et al.

2008). Major range shifts during prehistoric times and rapid colonization after agricultural declines in the East suggest that certain traits such as high genetic mobility via pollen may make some tree species better suited to adapting to climate change than many other plants (Hamrick 2004). However, late-successional conifers are poor dispersers and slow to respond to climate change (Neilson et al. 2005).

Forest composition may be slow to change, but many other effects of climate can be seen on forests around the world, including increased growth due to a longer growing season, faster growth rates particularly at higher elevations, increased water use efficiency, and increased growth from higher concentrations of CO_2 in the atmosphere. These changes are consistent with evidence that US forests have become more productive in the last 55 years (Boisvenue and Running 2006). Moreover, several studies have documented the upward movement of the alpine tree line and infilling of high-elevation meadows in western North America during the 20th century (e.g., Hessl and Baker 1997, Luckman and Kavanagh 2000). Climate change may reduce forest productivity due to increasing drought, temperature stress, and evapotranspiration, and indirect effects such as increased insect outbreaks, increasing prevalence of invasive species, and increased fire. Higher temperatures have likely caused recent increases in drought stress and forest die-offs through their influence on transpiration, carbon storage, insect populations, and host susceptibility (Allen et al. 2010). Global patterns suggest that seasonal droughts have induced dieback of deciduous trees while multi-year droughts are more likely the cause of coniferous dieback (Allen et al. 2010).

4.3.2   Projected trends
The IPCC predicts that overall forest growth in North America will likely increase 10–20% as a result of extended growing seasons and elevated CO_2 during the next century (Morgan et al. 2001) but with important spatial and temporal variations (Field et al. 2007). Forests in the ROCO region are expected to have less snow on the ground, a shorter snow season, a longer growing season due to an earlier spring start, earlier peak snow-

melt, and about two months of additional drought (fig. 7; Ray et al. 2008, Running 2009). Increased drought stress and higher temperatures may increase the likelihood of widespread die-offs (Breshears et al. 2005, Allen et al. 2010).

Dynamic vegetation models project that suitable habitat for western larch, whitebark pine, lodgepole pine, and subalpine fir is generally expected to decrease (Morrison in prep). A 3°C (5°F) temperature increase is expected to increase the growth of lodgepole pine in the northern part of its range, decrease growth in the middle, and decimate southern forests (Rehfeldt et al. 2001). In the coming century, subalpine forests are projected to decline in abundance and woodlands may become more abundant (fig. 5; Lenihan et al. 2008).

The key uncertainty regarding the future of forests lies in the interaction of multiple global change factors and the unpredictable nature of large disturbances such as fire and insect outbreaks. Researchers currently rely on models that link climate scenarios to vegetation dynamics and these are wrought with uncertainties. Such models are limited by the lack of local and accurate vegetation maps and appropriately scaled climate data (Allen et al. 2010). Moreover, it remains unclear if trees will keep pace with the rapidly changing climate through adaptation or by migrating to suitable habitat. Predictions are also hindered by an incomplete understanding of tree physiology, soil dynamics, and insect populations. Moreover, complex trophic interactions, which are not accounted for in these models, can drastically alter vegetation. For instance, warming may decrease predators, increase prey, and decrease the prey's preferred vegetation. Such a cascading effect has been documented in Isle Royale with wolves (*Canis lupus*), moose (*Alces alces*), and fir trees (Schmitz et al. 2003).

4.3.3   Five-needle pines
Five-needle pines such as limber pine and whitebark pine are keystone species that provide food and habitat for wildlife. Whitebark pine is found in upper subalpine ecosystems throughout the northern Rockies, where it often grows in areas with poor soils, high

winds, and steep slopes (Arno and Hoff 1990). The southern limit of its range is in the Greater Yellowstone Area (Little 1971). It provides food for more than 17 animal species, including the Clark's nutcracker (*Nucifraga columbiana)* and grizzly bear (*Ursus arctos horribilis)* (Arno and Hoff 1990). Limber pine is more widespread and occurs in the subalpine areas of the southern, central, and northern Rockies and in parts of the Upper Columbia Basin (e.g., Craters of the Moon National Monument and Preserve). Bristlecone pine, another five-needle pine, is found at high altitudes in the southern Rockies (Little 1971).

4.3.3.1   Observed trends

Whitebark pine has declined dramatically in the last century due to attacks by a blister rust fungus, epidemics of mountain pine beetles, fire suppression, and successional replacement, mainly by subalpine fir (Keane and Arno 1993, Kendall and Keane 2001). In areas where it was once a dominant feature of the landscape, it has declined by more than 50% and most of the remaining stands in the ROCO region are in high-elevation sites that have a limited capacity to produce

cones and regenerate (Kendall and Keane 2001). Mortality rates of whitebark pine populations in western Montana averaged 42% from the 1970s to the 1990s. With a large reduction in cone production and a decline in population size, whitebark pine is considered functionally extinct in more than a third of its range (Kendall 2010).

The primary cause of mortality has been white pine blister rust, a fungus native to Asia and now widespread across the West. The low natural resistance of North American five-needle pines along with favorable climatic conditions enabled the disease to spread rapidly. The pathogen became spread throughout the western white pine region in the early part of the 20th century and to higher elevations and a greater number of pine species more recently. It is now established in limber pine in Wyoming and Colorado, and bristlecone pine in southern Colorado. It was found for the first time in limber pine in Craters of the Moon in 2006, triggering concerns that the unique population on the lava flows may be at risk. In northwestern Montana and southern Alberta, surveys found that more than one-third of the limber

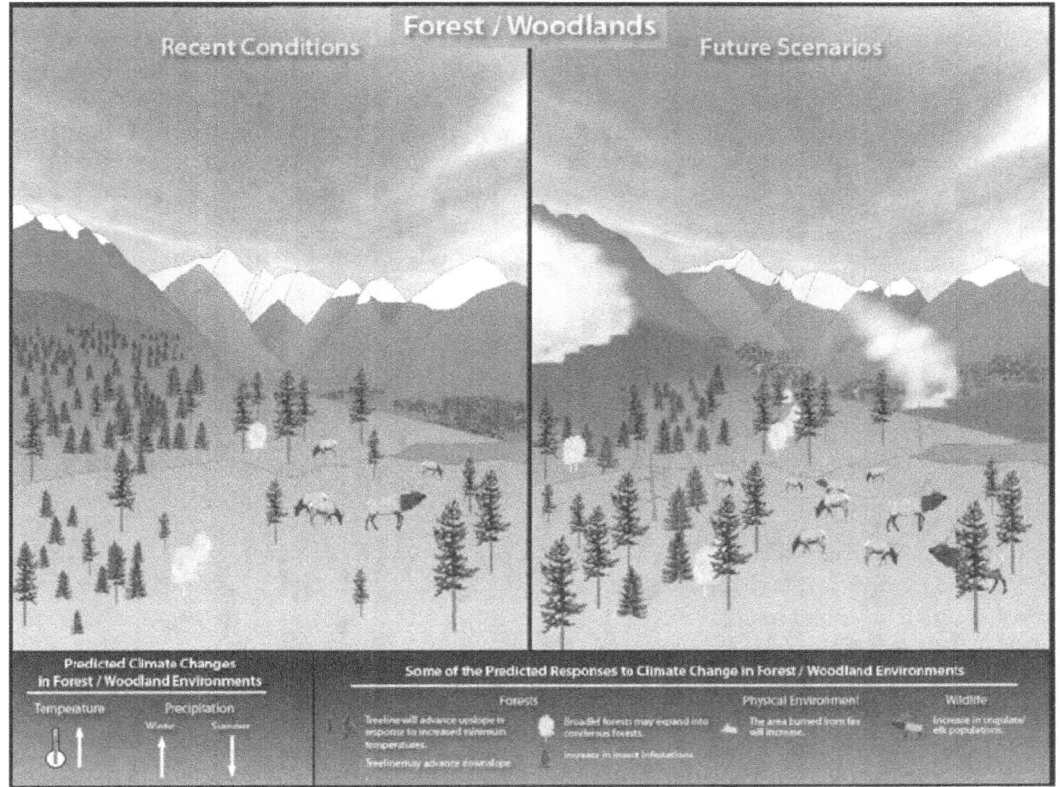

Figure 7. Conceptual diagram of projected changes for forests and woodlands.

pines were dead (Kendall et al. 1996).

Wind, temperature, and humidity can influence the dispersal of blister rust as can the availability of ribes (*Ribes* spp.) hosts (Van Arsdel et al. 2006). Generally, cool temperatures and high relative humidity favor disease spread and intensification. The incidence of pine infection may increase substantially during years when optimum environmental conditions coincide with spore production, dissemination, germination and infection (Koteen 1999). However, it is unclear whether climate change has had a role in driving blister rust because its impact does not seem to be constrained substantially by climate conditions across the Rockies. High humidity and warm weather provide better conditions for blister rust, but cold and dry conditions have not limited its spread to higher elevations in the Greater Yellowstone Area (Kendall and Keane 2001).

4.3.3.2   Projected trends
Regardless of climate, five-needle pines will likely continue to decline in the Rocky Mountains and the prevailing cause of death will continue to be blister rust. If five-needle pines are maintained in these ecosystems over the long term, they are expected to be very slow to respond to climate change and will alter their range northward or upslope. On the other hand, climate change may increase fire frequency, thereby reducing firs and other species that exclude five-needle pines, enabling expanded distributions in the future.

4.3.3.3   Summary
Climate is expected to play only a small role in the future of five-needle pines. It is likely, however, that widespread disease and mountain pine beetles will continue to devastate pine populations throughout the ROCO region.

4.3.4   Aspen
Aspen is the most widespread deciduous tree in North America (Little 1971). Its geographic range is limited to areas below 3,700 meters (12,139') (Mitton and Grant 1996) that receive more than 400 mm (16") of annual precipitation (DeByle and Winokur 1985). Aspen stands are patchily distributed in the ROCO region. It occurs in pure stands throughout the southern Rockies, but is less abundant in the northern Rockies, where it often occurs in smaller discrete patches (Stohlgren et al. 2002, Shepperd et al. 2001).

4.3.4.1   Observed trends
Aspen communities provide some of the most biologically diverse habitats in the intermountain West, where they help support an array of vascular plants in the understory as well as insects, birds, and mammals (Stohlgren et al. 2002). In particular, native ungulates use aspen as preferred forage and for shade and concealment. Aspen spreads primarily vegetatively in the West and clones can be very large. Individual stems within a clone are rarely live more than two centuries, and regeneration after fires is typically very strong (Sheppard et al. 2001a, b). Where aspen occurs in mixed stands, regeneration is limited in the shade of conifer species such as Douglas fir, subalpine fir, and juniper, and the aspen die after 100 to 150 years (Kaye et al. 2005). Aspen seedlings are rare but not uncommon after fires. One of the best known recruitment events was following the 1988 fires in Yellowstone National Park (Romme et al. 2005).

Widespread mortality of older aspen stems has occurred in the West in recent decades (Bartos 2001), but this decline has not been consistent across the landscape and regeneration of younger stems has been strong except where livestock and wildlife browsing is intense (Veblen et al. 2000). Declining stands in the West are associated with fire suppression, conifer encroachment, increased herbivory from elk, fungal infection, and sustained drought (Kashian et al. 2007). Heavy browsing by elk has reduced regeneration by 40–80% in Yellowstone National Park (Hart and Hart 2001) and by up to 90% in Rocky Mountain National Park (Binkley 2008). Aspen recruitment has been very limited since 1975 in areas of Rocky Mountain National Park with intensive elk grazing while remaining stable in areas with fewer elk, suggesting that herbivory plays a larger role than climate change in aspen decline (Binkley 2008).

While aspen is declining in some areas, other stands are persistent and increasing in size (e.g., Kashian et al. 2007). There has been a general increase in aspen in southern

Colorado since 1898, but patterns vary with elevation and fire history (Kukalowski et al. 2006). Aspen has been expanding upslope on southern exposures in the last century and this is thought to be due to climate warming (Elliott and Baker 2004). In Alberta, warmer temperatures and disturbance have led to seedling regeneration up to 200 meters (656') higher than the existing mature stands (Landhausser 2010).

4.3.4.2 Projected trends

As with other communities, aspen are influenced by many global changes in addition to warming temperatures. Experiments suggest that the growth of aspen is more accelerated by increased CO_2 concentrations than are other tree species (Lindroth 1993). On the other hand, ground-level ozone, which has been increasing in the West over the last century (Vingarzan 2004), has been shown to decrease aspen growth and photosynthetic rate and increase susceptibility to pests, but these effects are moderated when CO_2 is increased (Karnosky 2005). High mortality of lodgepole pine from mountain pine beetles may favor aspen growth, but this effect will likely only be seen in locations with existing aspen clones; it is unlikely to occur via seed recruitment (Romme et al. 2006). The future of aspen in national parks will be strongly dependent on elk management. After the 1988 fires in Yellowstone, seedling success was higher where ungulates were excluded (Romme et al. 2005). Ripple and Beschta (2004) have suggested a complex trophic relationship between wolf reintroduction, ungulates, and aspen and willow recovery that has implications for the long-term persistence of aspen in ROCO parks. Understanding and managing aspen in these areas will require consideration of the role of fire and elk browsing (Hessl 2002).

A recent paper examining sudden aspen decline and the impacts of global warming in the West forecasts that aspen will move upslope but will be lost from lower and drier areas (Rehfeldt 2009). The key uncertainties in forecasting the ecological response of aspen to climate change lies in our incomplete understanding of the causes of sudden die off, the long-term impacts of ungulate management, the potential appearance of non-

native insects or disease, and the interactive effects of other global changes.

4.3.4.3 Summary

Aspen forests are small in area but a vital resource in the West because of their high diversity and aesthetic appeal. While there has been some expansion of aspen into higher elevations and aspen may be positively affected by global changes such as increasing fire frequency, beetle outbreaks, and rising CO_2, aspen is expected to continue to decline at the landscape scale. In areas without hunting and large predators, including some national parks, the most important factor determining the success of aspen is increasing herbivore pressure. Aspen stand are expected to recover in parks that develop and implement elk management plans. As described by the Upper Columbia Basin Network, the desired condition for aspen in the parks is stands that exhibit adequate regeneration (>1200 stems/ha, 486/stems/acre), low levels of conifer encroachment, and canopy cover of >40%, and that do not have risks of die-off (Strand et al. 2009).

4.3.5 Summary

Climate change is expected to increase forest growth and many species will move upslope. Forest composition will likely change as once dominant species are eliminated from the community by disease and insect outbreaks and replaced by other tree species. Wildfires are predicted to increase in severity, frequency, and areal extent, which will have large impacts on stand age and structure. Dynamic vegetation models project a general decline in subalpine forests and an increase in woodlands at lower elevations.

4.4 Sagebrush and grasslands

Sagebrush and grasslands in the ROCO region include sagebrush steppe, represented in the western portions of the Great Northern LCC that border the Great Basin and in the Columbia Basin; shortgrass steppe, found in Colorado; Palouse grasslands, limited to eastern Washington and northwestern Idaho; and northern mixed grass prairie (Seastedt 2002). Other grasslands, such as subalpine meadows and those associated with ponderosa pine, are scattered throughout the foothills and higher elevations of the region. The intermountain sagebrush steppe and grasslands are a heterogeneous mixture of true grasslands, savannah, woodlands, and shrublands, and are strongly controlled by topographic moisture gradients (West and Young 2000). Presettlement fire intervals varied across the landscape from decadal in some moist grasslands in Colorado and mesic big sagebrush communities to 100 years or more in xeric sagebrush ecosystems (Bunting et al. 2002). Some of the most common native species in these communities are prairie Junegrass (*Koeleria macrantha)*, Idaho fescue (*Festuca idahoensis*), bluebunch wheatgrass (*Pseudoroegneria spicata*), rough fescue (*Festuca campestris*), Sandberg bluegrass (*Poa secunda*), threetip sagebrush (*Artemisia tripartite*), big sagebrush (*A. tridentate*), and blue grama (*Bouteloua gracilis*). Sagebrush steppe and grasslands in the ROCO region support sensitive wildlife species including black-footed ferrets, pronghorn antelope, sage grouse, and numerous sagebrush/grassland obligate songbirds (Knick et al. 2003, Aldridge et al. 2008).

4.4.1 Observed trends

Over the past 25 years, more than 25 million acres (10 million ha) of shrubland and grassland have been eliminated in the United States, twice the rate of forest loss (TNC 2009). Western shrublands and grasslands have been extensively modified by settlement, grazing, altered fire regimes, and introduced species, causing major, possibly irreversible, changes in ecosystem structure and function (e.g., Seastedt 2002, Knick et al. 2003). Many of the ROCO grasslands are currently managed as pasture. Sagebrush steppe is considered one of the most threatened US ecosystems (Noss et al. 1995). Cheatgrass is estimated to have invaded more than 50% of the sagebrush habitat in the Great Basin (Rowland 2006). One of the largest threats to western grasslands, particularly in Wyoming, is rapid energy development (e.g., oil, gas, and wind). Oil and gas development is expected to impact 3.7 million hectares (9.1 million acres) of sagebrush and 1.1 million hectares (2.7 million acres) of grasslands and reduce sage-grouse (*Centrocercus urophasianus*) populations

(Copeland et al. 2009). Biological invasions and habitat loss and fragmentation also pose major threats, and climate change will likely exacerbate their effects (Noss et al. 1995, Knick 2000, Knick et al. 2003, Aldridge et al. 2008).

There is evidence that warmer temperatures may promote the invasion of woodlands into grasslands, alter species composition and productivity, change herbivore pressure, and alter fire regimes. Pinyon-juniper woodland has increased an estimated 10-fold since the late 1800s (Miller and Tausch 2001), expanding into sagebrush and, to a lesser extent, other western grassland ecosystems (Miller et al. 2005). Climate change has been implicated in previous fluctuations in pinyon-juniper woodland extent (Soule et al. 2004). There is some evidence that woody species have also increased in subalpine grasslands, particularly in alpine-ecotones (e.g., Fagre 2009) and montane meadows (Berlow et al. 2002, Zier and Baker 2006).

Experimental work suggests that warming, particularly when coupled with drier conditions, can decrease sagebrush and grassland productivity and alter species composition (Poore et al. 2009). However, productivity is influenced by species diversity and grazing intensity (De Valpine and Harte 2001). Warming experiments in a montane grassland enhanced the growth of sagebrush compared to herbaceous species (Perfors et al. 2003). However, grasslands do not appear to be as responsive to warming as other community types such as tundra and forests (Rustad et al. 2001). Because grasslands are primarily limited by water and nutrient availability, an alteration in precipitation and fertilization may have larger effects than does temperature change (Parton et al. 1994). Changes in the frequency, duration, or quantity of precipitation can cause large changes in productivity, composition, and fire regimes (Knapp et al. 2002). Precipitation increases may favor invasive species. For example, increases in snow were shown to increase the invasion of forbs into mixed grass prairie (Blumenthal et al. 2008). The invasion of sagebrush steppe by cheatgrass has been shown to be strongly influenced by temperature and precipitation (Chambers et al. 2009). Climate variability has been shown to promote stability in grasslands by promoting the coexistence of different plant species (Adler et al. 2006). Increased atmospheric CO_2 may promote species compositional changes (Smith et al. 2000). There has been much work suggesting that rising CO_2 concentrations may differentially affect C3 and C4 grasses. These two pathways that plants use to capture CO_2 during photosynthesis correspond to other traits such as feed quality, production, and frost tolerance. Enrichment experiments in the shortgrass steppe have seen moderate increases in C3 grasses (Morgan et al. 2004) and a large increase in shrub biomass (Morgan et al. 2007). Weed invasion may also be driven by atmospheric CO_2 in semiarid ecosystems (Smith et al. 2000).

Large grazers and insect herbivores play a major role in structuring grassland communities. For instance, grasslands that evolved with large grazers, such as those east of the Rockies, have proved to be more resistant to invasion and degradation from cattle and development than have other areas (Mack 1986). Moreover, productivity is increased in grasslands where native grazers are present (Frank and McNaughton 1993). During a warming period 55.8 million years ago, insect damage to plants increased and was correlated with rising temperatures (Currano et al. 2008). A study in Yellowstone National Park found that drought caused a decline in belowground productivity and altered the effects of grazers (Frank 2007).

The best demonstrated effect of climate on grassland and sagebrush ecosystems is an indirect effect of fire. Large grassland fires typically follow a normal or wetter than usual summer the previous year and are more likely where exotic annual grasses are present (Knapp 1998). There is a well-established feedback loop in which fire promotes invasive grasses such as cheatgrass which promote more frequent fires (D'Antonio and Vitousek 2003). The cheatgrass-fire cycle has been a major factor in the loss of ecological integrity of sagebrush steppe ecosystems and, as previously discussed, climate change is likely to exacerbate a shift toward cheatgrass-dominated rangelands in the northern

portions of the ROCO region (Chambers et al. 2009, Bradley et al. 2009).

4.5 Projected trends

Over the short-term, the greatest threats to grasslands and sagebrush ecosystems come from oil and gas development, increasing urban and agricultural development, and invasive species. However, wildfires are increasing and likely to intensify in a warmer future with drier soils, longer growing seasons, and more severe droughts (Field et al. 2007), and these may cause large changes in grassland and sagebrush ecosystems (fig. 8). Direct impacts on big sagebrush, a keystone species throughout its range, may also be severe (Smith et al. 1997). The species is not fire tolerant and once removed from large disturbances, is very slow to recover (Smith et al. 1997). Weed invasion typically follows removal of sagebrush (Prevey et al. 2010), and this disturbance will likely be exacerbated by drought-induced stress on the species (e.g., Poore et al. 2009).

Modeling suggests that climate change will likely increase net primary production in grasslands and decrease soil carbon, but high annual variability in plant production makes these projections uncertain (Parton et al. 2005). Nutrient cycling and plant production are expected to occur more rapidly in response to climate change than changes in community composition (Parton et al. 1994).

Climate change is also expected to cause major changes in grassland and sagebrush distribution across the landscape (Bachelet et al. 2001). Range expansions of woody species are predicted to continue, particularly the expansion of pinyon-juniper into sagebrush steppe and grasslands (Rowland et al. 2008), resulting in a decrease in sagebrush and an increase in woodlands across the West. Changes in grassland cover are more subtle, but cover is generally predicted to decrease (Bachelet et al. 2001). Cremer et al. 1996, who used an earlier generation of downscaled global circulation models to predict the response of warming and reduced precipitation scenarios in eastern Washington, suggested that native sagebrush would decline and a less productive, invasive-an-

Figure 8. Conceptual diagram describing projected changes to sagebrush and grassland ecosystems.

nual dominated grassland would persist or increase. Such a shift has major implications for sagebrush-obligate vertebrates such as certain bird species (Knick et al. 2005). Climatic suitability models suggest that by 2100 sagebrush communities in Nevada, southern Idaho, Utah, Colorado, and eastern Wyoming may be at risk of loss due to climate change; regions in southwestern Wyoming will be at less risk (Bradley 2010).

There are a number of uncertainties in projecting the response of grasslands and sagebrush to climate change. First, regional, elevational, and grassland type may strongly influence response. A recent estimate of the velocity of climate change across biomes found that temperature changes will occur much more quickly in xeric shrublands and flooded grasslands than in other biomes, and much more slowly in montane grasslands (Laorie et al. 2009). Second, the magnitude and velocity of changes caused by the strong link between invasive species, fire, and grasslands and sagebrush is difficult to estimate. Third, precipitation and drought rather than temperature will likely drive changes in grasslands, and they are more difficult to

predict. Fourth, the future impact of grazers is difficult to estimate, particularly as grassland fragmentation increases. Finally, many grassland and sagebrush systems are actively managed through livestock grazing, invasive species control, and prescribed and suppressed fire.

4.5.1 Summary

Other immediate threats to grasslands and sagebrush such as invasive species and land use change appear to have outweighed the effects of climate change, but this assessment is likely to be modified if accelerated climate change continues. Observed changes over the last century and manipulative experiments suggest that warming, altered precipitation, and enhanced CO_2 can alter the productivity and diversity of grasslands. These effects are expected to continue, but the magnitude of changes may be small. Models project a large reduction in the distribution of sagebrush in the next century as it is converted to woodlands. Big sagebrush, the keystone species throughout much of the assessment area, is fire intolerant and appears to be vulnerable to both warming and drought, and is therefore likely to decrease throughout its range under climate change scenarios. However, the largest changes in sagebrush and grasslands are likely to occur where warmer temperatures and changing precipitation promote invasive species and altered fire regimes.

Chapter 5: Aquatic Systems

The ROCO region contains an abundance of glaciers, snowfields, lakes, streams, wetlands, rivers, and managed reservoirs that provide critical water resources to human and wildlife populations and support sensitive plant communities. High-elevation and snow-driven ecosystems such as those in the ROCO region are particularly sensitive to climate change and have seen a decline in freshwater resources (Field et al. 2007). Snowpack, which varies across the ROCO region but is typically greatest in high-elevation forests, peaks in early April and melts off during the summer, contributing an estimated 75% of the water in streams. High-elevation areas feed lower elevations through a network of lakes, streams, groundwater, and wetlands. Water levels and peaks in streamflow, which follow predictably from the pattern of snowmelt, are typically greatest in the spring and lowest in the fall. However, dams and reservoirs are common throughout the West and have significantly altered natural flow regimes.

Glaciers are common on the highest peaks of the ROCO region (Fountain 2006). Wyoming has the largest total area of glaciers (73.3 km²) in the region and the most glaciers (1,475), most of which lie within the Teton and Wind River Ranges. Montana has 1,158 glaciers covering 68.6 km²; Idaho has 208 (2.6 km²), and Colorado has 141 (4.8 km²) (Fountain 2006).

The ROCO region includes 26 stretches of river designated as "wild and scenic," most of them in Idaho (NWSR 2010). The numerous reservoirs and natural lakes managed for public water supplies and recreation vary from small alpine tarns to Flathead Lake in Montana, the largest natural freshwater lake in the West. Moving north through the ROCO region, the extent and volume of surface waters generally increases, following the prevailing precipitation gradient (fig. 1). These streams, lakes, and rivers are fundamental components of the western landscape and their ecology is intimately linked to the watersheds that they drain. Numerous species are dependent on these aquatic resources for part (e.g., aquatic invertebrates and amphibians), or all of their life cycle (e.g., freshwater fishes and aquatic plants). In addition, they provide a broad spectrum of ecological services, including nutrient processing, hydrologic cycling, and multiple socioeconomic functions for humans (e.g., water sources, fisheries, recreation, and irrigation).

Although they comprise less than 5% of the land area in the ROCO region (OTA 1993), wetlands are an integral component of its aquatic resources. They provide numerous important ecological functions by supporting biodiversity, increasing water and carbon storage, improving water quality, and providing wildlife habitat (Mitsch and Gosselink 2007). The most prevalent wetlands in the Rocky Mountains are associated with seepage slopes, river floodplains, surficial depressions, or the landforms associated with glacial retreat (Hauer et al. 1997).

There is much literature on how climate change may alter freshwater resources in the West (e.g., Ray et al. 2008, Williams et al. 2009, CIG 2010, Pederson et al. 2010); fig. 9). Here, we briefly summarize the observed and predicted changes in hydrology, surface water ecology, and wetlands. The effects of climate change on aquatic invertebrates, amphibians, and fish are discussed further in the wildlife section.

5.5.1 Observed trends

Changes to the hydrology in the West over the past 50 years due to climate change are well documented (Barnett et al. 2008), although land use, invasive species, agriculture, and increasing human demands have played a large role in determining trends in aquatic resources. In the northern and central Rockies, streamflows have shifted toward earlier peak runoff, which has been attributed to more precipitation falling as rain rather than snow and earlier snowmelt (Knowles et al. 2006, Hamlet et al. 2005; Mote 2005). Warmer and more variable winter and spring air temperatures (Sheppard et al. 2002, Abatzoglou and Redmond 2007) have accelerated melt and caused an overall decline in spring snowpack, particularly at lower elevations, despite increases in winter precipitation in many places (Mote et al. 2005, Field et al. 2007, Mote et al. 2008a, Ray et al. 2008). Reduced snowpacks have melted earlier and have advanced the timing of peak runoff by several days to weeks across much of the region (Stewart et al. 2005; Barnett et al. 2008). The most dramatic change in the past 50 years has been the decline of glaciers throughout the region. In 1993 the largest glaciers in Glacier National Park were measured at 72% of their 1850 areal extent and many small glaciers had vanished (Hall and Fagre 2003; Pederson et al. 2004). Although the distribution of lakes changed dramatically as the balance among precipitation, evapotranspiration, and runoff shifted during previous periods of climate change (Street and Grove 1979), a more recent change in lake distribution has not been reported for the region.

Changes in hydrological regimes have impacted the ecology of western aquatic resources (Barnett et al. 2008). For instance, warming temperatures may be contributing to the spread of the diatom *Didymosphenia geminate*, with more extensive nuisance growths becoming common in the region (Kumar et al. 2009). Another study documented that mayflies and other aquatic insects on which trout feed are emerging earlier and at smaller sizes in Rocky Mountain streams because of warmer streamflows and earlier peak runoff (Harper and Peckarsky 2006). Higher stream temperatures also affect fish access, survival, and spawning (Morrison et al. 2002; Keleher and Rahel 1996; Rieman et al. 2007; Williams et al. 2009). Increased wildfire activity has caused more debris flow events in streams with the potential to alter stream structure and function (Westerling et al. 2006; Morgan et al. 2008).

5.5.2 Projected trends

Climate change will significantly impact ROCO aquatic resources and will likely make it more difficult to achieve water quality standards nationwide (Field et al. 2007). While there are likely to be regional variations, projected effects across the West include loss of glaciers, less snow, earlier peak flows, less streamflow, warmer water temperatures,

more frequent droughts, and more intense storms (fig. 9).

At the current rate of melting, it has been suggested that the Glacier National Park's remnant glaciers will be gone in the next 25 to 30 years (Hall and Fagre 2003) due to increases in summer temperatures and a reduction in winter snowpack. Streamflow may increase during this initial period of melt, but flows will decline when the glaciers disappear (Morris and Walls 2009). Total winter precipitation may increase but overall snowpack is projected to decline throughout the West. For example, with a 4°C (7°F) temperature increase and doubling of atmospheric CO_2 in Loch Vale Watershed at Rocky Mountain National Park, models predict a 50% reduction in snowpack and 4–5 week earlier increases in soil moisture and runoff compared to mean onset of spring conditions from 1984 to 1998 (Baron et al. 2000b)

The loss of winter snowpack will greatly reduce the major source of groundwater recharge and summer runoff, resulting in a potentially significant lowering of water levels in streams, rivers, lakes, and wetlands during the growing season (Mote et al. 2005; Barnett et al. 2008). With warmer temperatures and increasing droughts, municipal and agricultural demands for water are likely to increase, drawing down freshwater resources even further (National Assessment Synthesis Team 2001). Lower summer base flows reduce the amount of instream habitat for invertebrates and fish and cause a reduction in stream-side groundwater tables which are important for sustaining riparian vegetation communities (Stromberg et al. 1996; Scott et al. 1999). Reduced water depths may also increase the vulnerability of sensitive species (e.g., amphibians) to harmful ultraviolet radiation (Kiesecker et al. 2001).

In addition to the shift in the quantity of water, climate change may reduce water quality due to increased erosion and decreased dilution of pollutants. Decreases in snow cover and more winter rain on bare soil are likely to lengthen the erosion season (Walker 2001), which could lead to average phosphorus concentrations in streams increasing 25 to 35% (Walker 2001). Predicted increases in

Figure 9. Projected climate changes to the hydrological cycle in the Rocky Mountains and Upper Columbia Basin.

the severity and frequency of floods may also contribute to increases in erosion, as well as affect ecological processes that are sensitive to changes in the probability distributions of high flow events such as habitat stability, biodiversity, and trophic structure (Konrad and Booth 2005, Hamlet and Lettenmaier 2007). Degradation of water quality will likely lead to a reduction in or loss of sensitive stream species (Waters 1995).

Warming air temperatures and a reduction in glacial inputs will lead to warmer water temperatures across the West. Surface and bottom water temperatures of lakes, reservoirs, rivers, and estuaries are projected to increase from 2 to 7°C (4–13°F) (Fang and Stefan 1998, 1999; Hostetler and Small 1999; Gooseff et al. 2005). Warmer waters may lead to oxygen depletion, a change in fish distribution, an increase in algae and zooplankton in coldwater lakes, and a loss of some species. Species that are isolated in habitats near thermal tolerance limits or that occupy rare and vulnerable habitats like alpine wetlands may become extinct (Williams et al. 2007), and fish such as trout that are dependent on cool waters will likely

decline (Williams et al. 2009; Pederson et al. 2010). In contrast, many fish species that prefer warmer water, such as largemouth bass and carp, may expand their ranges if surface waters warm (Battin et al. 2007). Warmer waters may also cause aquatic diseases and parasites to become more widespread (Hari et al. 2006).

5.1 Wetlands

Wetlands are among the most significantly altered ecosystems in North America due to stressors such as changes in hydrology from flow regulation, ground water pumping, fill placement, overgrazing by domestic and native ungulates, atmospheric deposition, and biological invasion (Patten 1998, Zedler and Kercher 2005). Over the last 200 years, wetland areas have declined approximately 56% in Idaho, 50% in Colorado, 38% in Wyoming, and 27% in Montana (OTA 1993). Like other freshwater ecosystems, wetlands are considered extremely vulnerable to climate change, which is projected to diminish their number and extent and cause a decline in associated flora and fauna (Field et al. 2007). Wetlands are already facing widespread degradation so that even small reductions in precipitation could exacerbate wetland loss.

A few of the wetland types considered at greatest risk globally are found in the ROCO region, including riparian wetlands in arid zones, peatlands, and alpine wet meadows (OTA 1993, Burkett and Kusler 2000). But despite the recognition of the increasing role of climate change in altering wetland functions (e.g., Baron et al. 2000b), there is a paucity of studies in the ROCO region that document climate-driven declines in wetland function or extent. One exception is a recent article describing changes in hydrology leading to wetland desiccation in Yellowstone National Park (McMenamin et al. 2008). Currently, the biggest losses are in the marshes on Yellowstone's northern range (Colorado State University, David Cooper, Research Scientist, email, May 2010). It is expected that loss of wetlands will result in a corresponding loss in biodiversity and critical functions such as carbon storage in peat and water storage (OTA 1993).

Warmer temperatures will affect the growth and reproduction of wetland species by increasing decomposition rates and evaporation from wetlands and their water supplies, reducing peat accumulation, and thawing upper layers of permafrost in alpine wetlands (Burkett and Kusler 2000, OTA 1993). Where warmer temperatures lead to increased fire severity and extent, peat bodies, particularly those in a matrix of forest, will be at risk. Where warmer temperatures cause an increase in wetland decomposition rates and reduce peat accumulation, carbon storage will be reduced.

Greater changes in wetlands are expected to result from altered precipitation as it affects soil and vegetation conditions (Winter 2000). Many models project wetter winters in the ROCO region, but any positive effect of increased winter flows for wetlands is expected to be outweighed by drier summers and warmer temperatures. It is predicted that wetlands response will first become evident in water table changes and alterations in the formation and duration of soil anoxic conditions. Alterations in the composition of short-lived and then longer-lived perennial plants will follow. Soils may be altered after

many decades unless fire occurs. Alterations of plant cover and soil permeability may act in a feedback loop to further modify the hydrological cycle. Some wetlands, such as forest wetlands and wet meadows, are particularly sensitive to hydrological changes and a reduction in the water table of a few inches could convert wetlands to upland habitats (Kusler 2006).

Reduced ground water flow due to lower snowpack, earlier melt dates, or reduced summer precipitation could result in lower water tables in wetlands dependant on ground water inputs (Poff et al. 2002). Riparian wetlands will be sensitive to precipitation because changes in the timing and magnitude of flooding will affect the flux of water, nutrients, sediment, and biota between main river channels and riparian wetlands (Hauer et al. 1997).

5.1.1 Summary

Climate change is a significant threat to the structure and function of US aquatic ecosystems. Changes in precipitation and warmer temperatures will have negative impacts on western water resources and there is high confidence that climate change will make it more difficult to maintain existing water quality due to warmer water temperatures and increasing erosion (Field et al. 2007). Warmer temperatures and earlier runoff will likely result in less available water for summer irrigation needs (Barnett et al. 2009, Knowles et al. 2006). Although rare, wetlands are hotspots of biodiversity and critical components of hydrological and biogeochemical cycles in the ROCO region. Wetlands have been reduced dramatically in the last century due to agriculture, development, and water management practices. It has only recently been recognized that climate change may also play a role in the loss of wetlands. Alpine wetlands, peatlands, and riparian corridors in arid regions may be particularly vulnerable.

While there is high confidence that climate change will alter freshwater ecosystems, numerous uncertainties exist. Many of the projected changes are based on precipitation changes, which are inherently more difficult to model than temperature. Moreover, the magnitude and frequency of extreme events such as droughts and floods are unpredictable, and these will have large impacts on water resources. The interacting effects of other stressors such as pollution, ultraviolet light, diseases, and environmental toxins with climate change are unknown. Moreover, the ramification of changes in food web structure and dynamics caused by the loss of some species and the expansion of others is unclear. Finally, and perhaps most importantly, the threat to water resources posed by increasing human demand is difficult to quantify.

The ROCO region is a diverse landscape with habitats ranging from alpine tundra to arid plains. Sparse settlement has left much of the habitat relatively intact and it is one of the last places in the continental United States with an intact assemblage of carnivores including gray wolves, grizzly bears, wolverine (*Gulo gulo*), and Canada lynx (*Lynx canadensis*). Within Colorado, Wyoming, Idaho, and Montana are 34 animal species listed as threatened or endangered, including gray wolves, Canada lynx, and grizzly bears, bull trout (*Salvelinus confluentus*), and black-footed ferrets (*Mustela nigripes*), and each of the four states has identified 200–300 species (about 10–20% of the fauna) as being of special management concern (CODoW 2009, IDFG 2009, MTNHP 2009, WGFD 2009). The taxa at the greatest current risk proportionally are freshwater fish and amphibians (IDFG 2009).

6.1.1 Observed trends

The abundance and diversity of wildlife in the West has declined due to severe hunting and trapping pressure in the past and land-use changes in more recent years. While hunting pressure has decreased since the early 1900s, development has accelerated. Increases in disturbance, fragmentation, and invasive species resulting from human development are a severe and immediate threat to wildlife in the ROCO region. Changes in climate, however, are already altering animal populations at global scales (Parmesan and Yohe 2003). There is evidence that warmer temperatures and changes in precipitation have caused range shifts, changes in population size, altered phenology, increases in disease prevalence, and altered migration patterns (Walther et al. 2002, Root et al. 2003). Moreover, climate change has indirectly affected animal populations through its effects on disturbance regimes, such as fire frequency, and the abundance and distribution of exotic species (Logan et al. 2003).

Some of the best documented effects of climate change on wildlife are from its effects on range size, population growth, and phenology. Range shifts have been well documented in a variety of species, including birds (see references in Parmesan 2006), butterflies (Crozier 2003, 2004, Forister 2010, Parmesan 1996), Odonata (dragonflies and damselflies) (Hickling et al. 2005), and small mammals (Moritz et al. 2008). Several of these species have moved their range upward in elevation as a result of warmer temperatures (Parmesan 1996, Parmesan and Yohe 2003). Concurrently, high elevations species such as pika have seen substantial range contractions (Moritz et al. 2008). Reduced precipitation, especially less snow, has created more favorable conditions for elk population growth in Montana (Creel and Creel 2009) and is predicted to improve conditions for elk in Colorado (Wang et al. 2002). Bats, which are difficult to study and generally under-represented in climate change assessments, are strongly controlled by environmental constraints on their physiology and tight energy budget (Humphries et al. 2002). Warming and altered precipitation under accelerated climate change are predicted to cause species range shifts and population declines, but no studies have documented recent shifts (Humphries et al. 2002, Adams and Hayes 2008). Changes in phenology and migration may cause asynchronies between wildlife populations and food sources, resulting in population declines, as has been seen for flycatchers (*Ficedula hypoleuca*) (Both et al. 2006). Asynchronies have developed for marmots and their food plants in the Rocky Mountains (Inouye et al. 2000), but there is no evidence of population declines. While there are many reports documenting the effects of climate change on wildlife in the ROCO region, they may not reflect the true effects of climate change because monitoring and research efforts are geographically and taxonomically biased (Joyce et al 2008). For instance, it appears from the literature that range expansions in birds may be the most common ecological consequence of climate change in the region (fig. 10), but other taxa are also presumably responding to climate change.

6.1.2 Projected trends

The IPCC predicts that climate change will continue to pressure species to shift their ranges northward and upward, causing a

Figure 10. Documented terrestrial wildlife response to observed changes in climate, based on 189 studies within the United States; none included Hawaii. From Joyce et al. 2008.

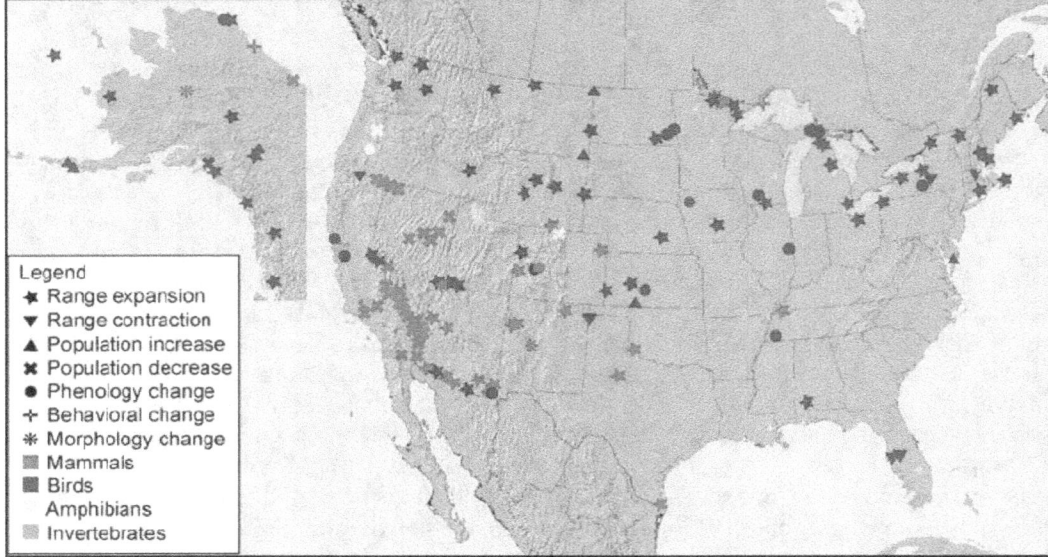

Legend
* Range expansion
▼ Range contraction
▲ Population increase
✱ Population decrease
● Phenology change
✛ Behavioral change
✳ Morphology change
▨ Mammals
■ Birds
  Amphibians
▨ Invertebrates

fundamental rearrangement of North American ecosystems (Field et al. 2007). While past warming was gradual, future change is expected to be more rapid and outpace wildlife's ability to adapt to new environments (Bradshaw and Holzapfel 2006). The magnitude and direction of species response to climate change will be highly variable and may differ among populations or regions (Parmesan 2006). For instance, small mammals in the West are more adapted to experiencing temperature variability in the southern parts of their range than in the northern parts, and this may buffer the effects of climate change in southern populations (Guralnick 2006). An analysis of potential climate change impacts on US national parks indicates that on average about 8% of current mammalian species diversity may be lost (Burns et al. 2003). The greatest losses are predicted to occur in rodent species (44%), bats (22%), and carnivores (19%) (Burns et al. 2003).

Although wildlife responses are expected to be complex and species-specific, several patterns can be projected based on life-history characteristics. First, highly mobile species with large geographic ranges, wide physiological tolerances, faster generation times, and generalist diets are more likely to adapt to a changing climate, while endemic specialists are projected to decline. For example, global change is generally predicted to increase the spread of invasive species (Dukes and Mooney 1999), and generalists such as

coyotes (*Canis latrans*) are expected to expand their range further north. Threatened and endangered species, particularly those with low genetic diversity, small population sizes, and narrow ranges, will be increasingly threatened by climate change. As an example, bull trout, which are dependent on cool water temperatures, are expected to continue to decline and populations will be restricted to high elevations (Rieman et al. 2007). Bats are considered susceptible to climate change because of their slow reproduction rate, sensitivity to roost temperatures and water availability close to their roosts, and dependency on the availability of large insect populations (e.g., Adams and Hayes 2008).

Second, species that are currently limited by temperature or precipitation are likely to respond more quickly to climate change than are other species. While disease and invasive species are driving a decline in the abundance and diversity of freshwater fish and amphibians in the ROCO region, these species' sensitivity to warming temperatures is a contributing factor. Snow-dependent species such as wolverine, lynx, and snowshoe hare (*Lepus americanus*) are considered particularly vulnerable to climate change. For example, modeling of potential future climate and subsequent changes in vegetation and snow cover indicates that potential lynx habitat may decrease significantly by 2100 (Gonzales et al. 2007). Wolverines are dependent on persistent spring snow cover for successful denning and, as climate warms, fewer sites will be suitable, connectivity among sites will decrease, and there may be substantial loss in the wolverine's range (Copeland et al. 2010).

Third, climate change is expected to alter the distribution of vegetation, which will alter the availability of wildlife habitat. Several community types are likely to greatly decrease in area, including alpine, subalpine spruce-fir, and sagebrush (fig. 5; Lenihan et al. 2008; evidence from sagebrush bird declines supports this contention (Knick et al. 2003, Aldridge et al. 2008). Climate-driven losses of high-elevation habitat are expected to contribute to declines of many mammals including grizzly bears, bighorn sheep, pikas, mountain goats, and wolverines (GAO 2007). Similarly, movement patterns of deer, bighorn sheep, and elk may be affected temporally as snowpack patterns shift (Janetos et al. 2008). A projected 60–90% loss of suitable bird habitat is predicted to decrease neotropical migratory bird species richness 30–57% during the next century (Price and Root 2005).

Above, we have described in general terms the recent and predicted trends of wildlife responses to climate change in the ROCO region. We now highlight select species or taxa that are of particular concern to land managers or may be especially good indicators of the broader effects of climate change. These case studies include fish, amphibians, birds, pika, invertebrates, ungulates, and grizzly bears.

6.1 Fish

Of the roughly 800 native freshwater fishes in the United States, only about 21% are found in the West. However, the ROCO region contains many threatened or endangered fish, including greenback cutthroat (*Oncorhynchus clarki stomias*), bull trout, pike minnow (*Ptychocheilus lucius*), several species of salmon, and white sturgeon *(Acipenser transmontanus)* (CODoW 2009, IDFG 2009, MTNHP 2009, WGFD 2009).

Warmer stream and lake temperatures and changing streamflow will affect fish access, survival, and spawning (Morrison et al.

2002). While climate change is expected to have a large impact on all native fish, trout and salmon will likely fare worse than many because of their dependency on cool, clear water and because they have narrow thermal tolerances (Williams et al. 2007). Salmonids may provide an early indicator of climate change in the ROCO region (Pederson et al. 2010), where warming is projected to cause a loss of up to 42% of current trout and salmon habitat by the end of the century and losses of western trout populations may exceed 60% (Keleher and Rahel 1996). Losses of migratory bull trout may be as high as 90% (Rieman et al. 2007). In addition to the direct effect of warmer water temperatures, fish populations will be indirectly affected by warmer waters promoting the expansion of aquatic invasive or nuisance species such as *Didymosphenia geminate* (Kumar et al. 2009) and invasive aquatic plants which can alter food web dynamics and oxygen availability. Aquatic invertebrates, which are the primary food source for trout and fish, will be affected where climate causes earlier emergence, species loss, or smaller size (Harper and Peckarsky 2006). Changes in streamflow and fire regimes will also likely contribute to habitat loss (Pederson et al. 2010).

6.2 Amphibians

Amphibians are likely to be highly sensitive to climate change (Blaustein et al. 2001; Carey and Alexander 2003; Corn 2005; Lawler et al. 2010b) and have been identified as one of the taxonomic groups showing early responses to it (McCarty 2001; Walther et al. 2002). Within the Western hemisphere, amphibians are predicted to experience more range shifts than either birds or mammals (Lawler et al. 2009). Climate change is expected to have large effects on amphibians because as ectotherms, all aspects of their physiology and life history are strongly influenced by their physical environment. Direct effects of climate change on amphibians include changes in movements, phenology, and physiological stress. Indirect effects include changes in predators, competitors, food supply and habitat (Donnelly and Crump 1998), and invasive species, e.g., bullfrogs (Ficetola et al. 2007). The documented and anticipated impacts of climate change on amphibians vary according to species-specific life history traits and although generally considered detrimental, may in limited cases by beneficial (McCarty 2001; Werner et al. 2009). Region-specific empirical data are limited, but below we briefly review some of the general concepts of how climate change may affect amphibians in the ROCO region.

Precipitation has a strong influence on amphibian abundance, activity and migration. Populations of several species have declined dramatically in years of drought (Stewart 1995; Pounds and Crump 1994). Low precipitation or drought can decrease the amount of available wetland breeding habitat, reduce water depth thereby exposing amphibian embryos to more extreme water temperatures, and increasing the potential for pond drying before metamorphosis occurs. Climate change also has the potential to fragment amphibian habitat and result in dry open areas that are barriers to dispersal (Dodd and Smith 2003). Gibbons and Bennett (1974) reported that activity patterns among 16 frog species were positively correlated with the incidence of precipitation, and it is generally thought that precipitation increases the ability of amphibians to move across the landscape. Species associated with ephemeral waters, including shallow ponds and intermittent streams, may be particularly vulnerable to altered precipitation patterns. Amphibian monitoring in Grand Teton and Yellowstone national parks showed that in 2007 and 2008 the majority of amphibian breeding sites were in temporary or seasonally flooded wetlands and the minority were in saturated or semi-permanent wetlands (Patla et al. 2009). McMenamin et al. (2008) documented an increase in the number of permanently dry ponds in Yellowstone's Lamar Valley over a 16-year period and a concomitant reduction in the number of remaining wetlands that were occupied by amphibians (but see Patla et al. 2009). However, the documented and anticipated effects of climate change on amphibians are not all detrimental. Werner et al. (2009) found that drought greatly reduced pond hydroperiods and caused a corresponding decrease in predator densities, which lead to increased colonization probability and decreased extinction probability for chorus frogs (*Pseudacris triseriata*).

Temperature also exerts a strong influence on amphibian survival and reproduction. Environmental temperature affects growth rates, time to reach metamorphosis, mechanisms of gas exchange, and rates of energy metabolism (Ultsch et al. 1999). Amphibians use behavioral and physiological mechanisms for thermoregulation but are limited by their need for water (Hutchison and Dupre 1992). The temperature tolerance of anuran larvae is a key factor in determining the species' range limits. Kiesecker et al. (2001) found that ENSO events in the Pacific Northwest resulted in low winter precipitation, and in the spring following an ENSO event, boreal toad (*Bufo boreas*) embryos developed in shallower water and had greater mortality than in wetter years when embryos developed in deeper water. In years with low precipitation, infection of toad embryos by the pathogenic fungus *Saprolegnia ferax* was >50% at water depths <20cm. Furthermore, Kiesecker and Blaustein (1995) documented that boreal toad embryos are only susceptible to *S. ferax* in the presence of UV-B radiation. However, in a related study, Corn and Muths (2002) found that earlier breeding during dry years minimized exposure to UV-B due to shallow water depths; they proposed extreme water temperatures as an alternative or additional plausible hypothesis to explain the high mortality of boreal toads observed by Kiesecker et al (2001). Still, these studies suggest that climate change has the potential to increase the prevalence of infectious disease.

Chytridiomycosis is a potentially lethal disease caused by the amphibian chytrid fungus (*Batrachochytrium dendrobatidis*) that has been implicated in population declines of several amphibian species throughout the world (Daszak et al. 1999; Carey 2000; Muths et al. 2008). Several studies suggest that climate change may enable the fungus to expand its range due to warmer temperatures and moisture at higher elevations (Bosch et al. 2007; Pounds et al. 2006). Boreal toads appear to have experienced a population decline across the Rocky Mountains from north to south, a pattern potentially associated with the distribution of chytrid fungus. Muths et al. (2008) found that the fungus is widespread in the Rocky Mountains from northern Montana to southern Colorado.

The fungus was found at a higher proportion of low-elevation boreal toad breeding sites, and results from this study suggested that the distribution of chytrid fungus is limited by temperature, which is moderated in the higher elevations. Increased temperatures associated with climate change are likely to allow the expansion of chytrid fungus into high elevation areas.

Climate change has been associated with phenological changes in several amphibian species. Beebee (1995) documented earlier breeding correlated with increasing temperatures since the 1970s for two species of frogs and four salamanders in Britain. However, in montane habitats winter snow accumulation is more important than temperature in predicting the behavior of amphibians (Inouye et al. 2000; Corn and Muths 2002). Corn (2003) found a strong correlation between timing of breeding and both snow water equivalent and air temperature for amphibians in the Pacific Northwest. Although some studies have not found significant changes in amphibian breeding phenology, Beebee (2002) suggested that interspecies differences in reproductive biology might explain differing responses to warming temperatures. In Britain, the "explosive" breeders that spawn early in the year have shown minimal signs of response to climate change, whereas the later and more protracted breeders, which include urodeles or salamanders, have bred progressively earlier over the past 20 to 30 years (Beebee 2002).

In summary, the effects of climate change on amphibians are expected to be multi-faceted and include direct physiological impacts as well as indirect impacts to the species' habitat, competitors, predators, and pathogens.

6.3 Invertebrates

The population size and range of numerous species of mollusks, amphipods, butterflies, and aquatic invertebrates have declined in the last century, and invertebrates now make up roughly half of the species of special concern in Colorado, Idaho, Wyoming, and Montana despite being one of the least well-studied taxa (CODoW 2009, IDFG 2009, MTNHP 2009, WGFD 2009). Invertebrate declines are attributed to a variety of causes, including land use, invasive species, changing food web dynamics, and climate change. However, some invertebrates are increasing their geographic range and population size in response to climate change, as has been seen for disease vectors like ticks and mosquitoes (Field et al. 2007). This is not surprising because invertebrates, which are ecotherms, are generally expected to increase activity and reproduction in warmer temperatures. Their short generation times also increase the capacity of invertebrates to adapt to changing conditions (Parmesan 2006). For many species of invertebrates, however, drought and changing biotic interactions have outweighed any positive effects of warmer temperatures, and evolutionary responses to climate change are not occurring rapidly enough to prevent extinctions (Parmesan 2006).

Aquatic insect assemblages are thought to be particularly vulnerable to climate change, and experiments support the expectation that the structure and function of these communities will be altered (Hogg and Williams 1996). For example, as alpine stream temperatures rise and flow regimes change, rare, cold-water-obligate, aquatic invertebrate species may be driven to extinction (Hauer et al. 1997). Higher water temperatures can increase the rate of microbial activity and decomposition of organic material, which may result in less food being available for invertebrates (Meyer and Edwards 1990). Moreover, warmer temperatures will allow many lower-elevation invertebrates to colonize alpine streams and lakes, causing changes in food-web dynamics (Hauer et al. 1997).

Terrestrial invertebrates are also likely to be responsive to climate change. Endemic insects that have limited home ranges, such as the Great Sand Dunes tiger beetle (*Cicindela theatina*), may be sensitive to loss of habitat in a warmer, drier climate. Pollinators such as bees may be at risk where plant composition and phenology changes; asynchronies between insects, pollinators, and flowering plants have been documented (Visser and Both 2005). The best evidence of the ecological response of invertebrates to climate change comes from butterflies. Many populations of Edith's checkerspot butterfly

(*Euphydryas editha*) in the western United States, Canada, and Mexico have gone extinct in the last century and extinction rates were significantly lower at high elevations and high latitudes (Parmesan 1996). Alpine butterflies are particularly vulnerable to changes in climate because their brief life cycle is highly correlated with the melting of snow and increasing summer temperatures (McLaughlin et al. 2002). For the alpine butterfly, encroaching forests into meadows may reduce dispersal and gene flow among populations (Roland and Matter 2007). During the last 35 years there has been a general trend for butterfly species richness to decline and an upward migration of butterfly ranges in California (Forister et al. 2010).

At this point, it is difficult to distinguish among the effects of climate change, land-use change, and other stressors on invertebrate populations. However, despite relatively fast generation times, it is clear that many invertebrates are sensitive to climate and species with isolated or rare populations may be particularly vulnerable.

6.4 Birds

Birds have been suggested as ideal early indicators of climate change (Berthold et al. 2004; Fiedler 2009; Niven et al. 2009) because they are sensitive to weather and climate and are generally easy to detect, identify, and count, and much knowledge base exists regarding their life history and population trends. Because they are well-studied and include both widespread and geographically restricted species, they are considered an ideal class of organisms with which to investigate and test the current and predicted impacts of climate change.

More is known about the responses of birds to climate change than any other group of animals (Wormworth and Mallon 2008) and the evidence that recent climate change has already begun to affect birds is compelling. Almost all aspects in the life cycle of birds that have been studied so far show recent changes that can be linked to climate change, including the declining size of North American birds (Van Buskirk et al. 2010). Avian responses to climate change can be broadly categorized as changes in range

and distribution, phenology, behavior, and morphology (Fiedler 2009; Van Buskirk et al. 2010). Weather conditions are known to affect avian metabolic rates (e.g., cold weather increases the energy expenditure necessary for body maintenance), the abundance and distribution of their prey, and their ability to forage, migrate, and carry out courtship behaviors. Extreme weather events such as prolonged freezes or droughts can have catastrophic effects on juvenile and adult birds (Schreiber and Schreiber 1984; Stenseth et al. 2002). Climate change is anticipated to affect the staging, stopover ecology, and fuelling of migratory birds (DEFRA 2005).

Documentation of range shifts was employed early on to detect the ecological effects of climate change (Vitousek 1992). Documented changes in bird ranges and distribution are numerous and include both altitudinal (Pounds et al. 1999) and latitudinal shifts in breeding ranges (Hitch and Leberg 2007) and wintering ranges (La Sorte and Thompson 2007; Sekercioglu et al. 2008). Niven and colleagues (2009), who analyzed Christmas bird count data (1966–67 through 2005–06) to estimate population trends for North American bird species, found a significant northern shift in the latitudinal center of abundance in 177 of 305 species (overall mean shift = 56 km, 35 mi) coincident with a positive increase in monthly temperature over the 40-year period. Among the four habitat-based guilds they investigated, woodland birds, shrubland birds, and generalists showed significant shifts, while grassland birds did not. Further evidence that climate change is likely to be the cause of these range shifts is provided by Root (1988), who found that the entire length of the northern range limits of 62 species wintering in the conterminous United States and southern Canada was tightly associated with a particular average minimum January temperature isotherm.

Substantial empirical evidence of range shifts occurring in the late 20th century (citations above and Walther et al. 2002; Parmesan and Yohe 2003; Root et al. 2003; Parmesan 2006) confirms that a widespread ecological response to climate change is underway. Consequently, researchers are transitioning from documenting range shifts to attempting to forecast them (La Sorte and Jetz 2010). There is also a focus on improving predictions of extinction risk related to climate change (Shoo et al. 2005). Sekerciouglu et al. (2008) found that elevational limitation of range size explained 97% of the variation in the probability of 8,459 species of Western Hemisphere landbirds being in a World Conservation Union category of extinction risk. Many highland taxa will likely experience population decreases as climate change forces them to move to higher elevations (Pounds et al. 1999; Shoo et al. 2005). To improve the precision of estimates of climate-induced extinction risk, high-resolution (<1 km, 0.6 mi) data on elevational limit shifts (Sekerciouglu et al. 2008) and spatial patterns of abundance within a species distribution are needed (Shoo et al. 2005).

Phenological responses of birds to climate change are well documented, including earlier migration (Inouye et al. 2000; Sparks et al. 2005), development of partial migration (only part of a bird population migrates; Fiedler 2003), and earlier breeding (Crick et al. 1997; Dunn and Winkler 1999). Climate warming can cause negative impacts migration and breeding are no longer synchronized with the timing of peak resources. According to the phenology mismatch hypothesis, migrant birds that experience a greater rate of warming in their breeding grounds than their wintering grounds are likely to experience population declines because their migration will occur later and they may miss the beginning of the breeding season. Population trends are also expected to be negatively associated with migration distance because the potential for phenology mismatch increases with the number of staging sites. Jones and Cresswell (2010), who examined population and temperature trends in the wintering and breeding areas for 193 spatially separate migrant bird populations, found that phenology mismatch was correlated with population declines in the Nearctic, whereas migratory distance was more important in explaining population declines in the Paleaeartic. These results suggest that differential global climate change may already be contributing to the decline of some species, and the effect may be more important in the Nearctic. Furthermore,

climate change is generally expected to be a greater threat to long-distance migrants than to resident species, and to species breeding in more strongly seasonal habitat (Winkler et al. 2002).

In association with earlier breeding (Crick et al. 1997), clutch sizes have increased and nesting success has declined for some species (Both et al 2006). While earlier arrival at breeding sites and earlier onset of egg laying could lead to larger clutch sizes for some species, reduced survival of post-fledging birds may prevent these populations from increasing (Fiedler 2009). For example, Both et al. (2006) showed that populations of a small passerine had reduced nesting success and declined because the phenology of their main food supply during breeding had advanced faster than the birds' breeding date.

Almost all aspects in the life cycle of birds that have been studied so far show recent changes that can be linked to climate change. While relatively few studies have been conducted within the ROCO region, the responses of birds to climate change there are expected to be similar to those documented elsewhere. Generally speaking, birds with restricted ranges or bounded distributions (e.g., mountain-top species), poor dispersal ability, and small population size are most at risk of extinction. Species within the ROCO region that are known to be at heightened risk of extinction due to climate change are alpine birds such as rosy finches and ptarmigan.

Because they are easy to detect, identify and count, are well-studied and include both widespread and geographically restricted species, birds have been suggested as ideal early indicators of climate change (Berthold et al. 2004; Fiedler 2009; Niven et al. 2009).

6.5   Pika

The American pika is a small mammal related to rabbits and hares (Order Lagomorpha) that lives in montane rocky environments of western North America from British Columbia to the southern Great Basin (Smith and Weston 1990). In the ROCO region, pika can be found in lava flows at low elevations and in talus slopes of high alpine environments

(Smith and Weston 1990). Over the last century, local populations in the Great Basin have disappeared coincident with warming temperatures (Beever et al. 2003, Beever et al. 2010), and their range in California has contracted and moved to higher elevations (Moritz et al. 2008).

Pikas are suspected of being particularly vulnerable to climate change for a number of reasons. First, they are physiologically unable to survive high temperatures without access to cooler microclimates such as talus fields, which offer sub-surface temperatures several degrees cooler than shaded locations at the surface (MacArthur and Wang 1974, Millar and Westfall 2010) and high temperatures can limit foraging. Second, some populations of pika are snow-dependent because snowpack serves as insulation in winter months for active pikas in alpine regions (Morrison and Hik 2007). Where snowpack is reduced, pikas may die of exposure to low temperatures, and evidence for snowpack-demographic correlations has been described (Kreuzer and Huntly 2003, Morrison and Hik 2007, Beever et al. 2010). Finally, pika populations are restricted to isolated talus or lava flows and it is thought that they have low dispersal capacity (Hafner and Sullivan 1995).

Recent models predict that high-elevation pika habitats will see significant warming (Ray et al. 2010). Genetic evidence shows a very strong climate signal for Holocene range contractions (Galbreath et al. 2009). A recent study in Craters of the Moon showed that the species was restricted to the park's highest elevation lava flows (Rodhouse et al. 2010), suggesting that range shifts may occur along an elevational gradient, reflecting the direct impacts of temperature and precipitation. The US Fish and Wildlife Service, however, concluded that the best available scientific information indicates that pikas will be able to survive despite higher temperatures and will have enough suitable high elevation habitats to prevent them from becoming threatened or endangered (USFWS 2010). Recent evidence suggests that many populations in the western Great Basin and Sierra Nevada are thriving (Millar and Westfall 2010), although the same study found the

species to be elevationally restricted in other portions of the Great Basin. In summary, pikas are vulnerable to climate change but the magnitude of climate effects varies regionally and more research is needed to understand the future of pika populations in a warmer climate.

6.6   Ungulates

The ecology of ungulates in the ROCO region is strongly influenced by climate. Summer precipitation, winter snow pack, and the timing of spring green-up affect their physiology, demography, diet, habitat selection, and predator-prey interactions. Ungulate body size and mortality have been shown to follow patterns of climate variability (Post and Stenseth 1999). For instance, moose survival has been linked to temperature and, in the southern areas of its range, warmer temperatures combined with high humidity may cause populations to decline (Lenarz et al. 2009). It is unclear whether the large increases in moose population in Colorado since its reintroduction in 1978 (Vieira 2006) is due to climate. The degree of response to climate change from species such as elk, moose, mule deer, and white-tail deer, and pronghorn antelope is uncertain. Some species such as pronghorn are threatened most by land-use change.

Ungulates dependent on high-elevation habitats, such as mountain goats and bighorn sheep, are expected to decline in response to warmer temperatures and habitat loss (GAO 2007). Glacier National Park has lost about 4% of its alpine zones to trees because of a warming climate, and this threatens mountain goat populations by reducing forage, providing shelter for predators, and fragmenting habitat (Fagre 2009). Bighorn sheep populations are inversely correlated with elk population size and are particularly sensitive to reductions in precipitation (Picton 1984). One of the key issues for ungulate management is wildlife disease, the spread and virulence of which is likely to be exacerbated by climate change (Harvell et al. 2002). Species such as bighorn sheep that are particularly sensitive to disease may be threatened.

While some ungulates populations will decrease in a warmer climate, others that are currently limited by winter mortality may increase as winter snowpack declines. As discussed earlier, elk populations in Montana and Colorado are expected to increase as winters become less severe and forage plants increase in productivity (Wang et al. 2002, Creel and Creel 2009).

6.7 Grizzly bears

The grizzly bear *(Ursus arctos horribilis)* is a subspecies of brown bear that once roamed the mountains and prairies of the West. Between 1800 and when the species was listed as threatened in 1975, grizzly populations south of Canada plummeted from 50,000 animals to fewer than 1,000 (Tomback and Kendall 2002). Today, the grizzly bear remains in a few isolated locations in the lower 48 states, including the Greater Yellowstone Area and parts of northern Montana and Idaho, where active recovery management has increased populations during the last two decades (Schwartz et al. 2006, Kendall et al. 2009). Current mortalities are primarily caused by human activity and population densities are generally inversely related to human population (Schwartz et al. 2006, Kendall et al. 2008, Ciarniello et al. 2009).

Bear populations may decline as winter ungulate mortality decreases as a result of warmer temperatures and shorter winters (Schwartz et al. 2006) and because of projected declines in the availability of whitebark pine seeds (Kendall and Keane 2001). In the Greater Yellowstone Area, the frequency of captures of problem grizzly bears increases sixfold and bear mortality rates are two to three times higher during years of low whitebark pine seed production (Mattson and Reinhart 1997). Reductions in other important food sources such as native trout, army cutworm moth, and huckleberries as a result of warmer, drier conditions may contribute to grizzly decline. In a warmer climate, grizzly bears may increasingly rely on exotic species that are considered less nutritious than native food sources (Reinhart et al. 2001). In the Greater Yellowstone Area, males bears have shown later den entrance dates (Haroldson et al. 2002), and denning times are expected to be shorter as temperatures rise. Interactions with humans are expected to increase with land use changes, decreased denning, and declining food sources.

It is unclear how climate change will affect grizzly bear populations. Through its effects on fire, insect outbreaks, and plant disease, climate will indirectly affect the food sources of bears and their potential for interacting with humans, and this could threaten their future. However, grizzly bears are highly mobile and generalist omnivores, two characteristics that suggest they will not be as sensitive to climate change as other wildlife. They may adapt to changing conditions, move to new areas and new food sources, and maintain their population sizes under a warmer climate.

6.7.1 Summary

There are numerous uncertainties involved in predicting wildlife responses to climate change, the largest being that associated with vegetation change. Shifts in vegetation and habitat availability, whether caused by climate or land use change, will have strong impacts on wildlife populations. Another uncertainty results from the lack of the basic life-history data needed to estimate vulnerability. How biotic interactions will be altered and to what degree this will affect populations remains unknown. Phenotypic plasticity and behavior adaptations may allow species to respond to change in unpredictable ways. The responses of wildlife to nonclimate stressors such as fire, disease, and invasive species may dampen or strengthen responses to climate change.

There is evidence that warmer temperatures and changes in precipitation have caused range shifts, asynchronies, altered migration and hibernation patterns, increases in disease prevalence, and ultimately a reduction in the population size of many species (Walther et al. 2002, Root et al. 2003). Moreover, climate change can strongly affect animal populations through its effects on disturbance regimes, disease, land use, and invasive species. The predicted responses of wildlife to climate change are that:

- Many species' ranges will move northward and upward in elevation.

- Species will respond differentially, creating non-analog communities and asynchronies among interacting species.

- In most cases, climate changes will be more rapid than evolutionary adaptations.

- Species that are mobile, genetically diverse, show wide physiological tolerances, and have generalist diets will respond the most positively.

- Temperature-limited and snow-adapted species are at particular risk to a changing climate.

- Wildlife associated with habitat types and communities such as spruce-fir, alpine and sagebrush that are expected to decline are at greater risk.

Chapter 7: Conclusions

Climate change is having significant effects on organisms and ecosystems throughout the ROCO region. Although uncertainties remain, for many processes and resources there is published evidence of observed responses to climate change within the last century and well-developed hypotheses and models that project a continued response during the next decade. This report provides a synthesis of information available as of March 2010, but because of the diversity of topics addressed and rapid progress in climate change science, we are sure to have missed some relevant literature.

We found that surface waters, glaciers, alpine communities, wetlands, fire regimes, wildlife and plant disease, narrowly endemic species, and freshwater fish are particularly responsive or vulnerable to climate change and may be useful indicators for the ROCO region. For many other ecological properties and processes, communities, and species, non-climate stressors such as pollution and habitat loss, are anticipated to drive changes over the next century. For instance, grasslands and sagebrush are extremely vulnerable to changes in fire regimes and biological invasions. Still, other systems and resources may respond to climate change by increasing population size and range. In many cases, we lack published evidence that link recent trends in a resource to climate change, but well-developed hypotheses suggest that the resource may be vulnerable in the future. For example, it is projected that bats and moun-

Table 2. Inventory, monitoring, and research needed to better understand ecological responses to climate change in the Rocky Mountains and Upper Columbia Basin.

Inventory, Monitoring, and Research Needs

Climate and Air Quality

Inventory & Monitoring
- Increase climate monitoring at high elevations.
- Create baseline climate records that are appropriately QA/QC'ed for long-term trends and variability analyses.
- Increase geographic coverage of air quality and visibility monitoring in remote areas.
- Monitor sensitive ecosystems for air pollution effects (e.g., species composition changes due to N deposition, ozone injury to plants in riparian or sagebrush areas).

Research
- Downscale global and regional climate models to local and watershed scales.
- Conduct research on how N deposition and its ecological effects will change in a warming climate.
- Incorporate information on fire emissions, particulate matter concentrations, and visibility effects into fire management plans and models of fire effects.
- Examine the effects of energy development on ground-level ozone concentrations
- Improve region-wide atmospheric and ecosystem modeling to predict the effect of climate change on air quality and the resources sensitive to it.

Ecological Processes

Inventory & Monitoring
- Monitor key taxa or communities that are considered to be at risk of extinction.
- Monitor forest and grassland productivity across precipitation gradients.
- Compile, analyze, and report on historical phenological records in the western United States.
- Develop a phenology monitoring program and identify key taxa to monitor from the National Phenology Network or based on availability of historical data, projected response to climate change, or ease of measurement

Research
- Research wildlife migration and dispersal, habitat-use, and metapopulation dynamics to aid in prioritizing management actions and documenting climate-driven changes.
- Focus on the differential effects of climate change on interacting species to identify asynchronies and mismatches.
- Conduct vulnerability assessments on communities and taxa (or groups of taxa such as tropical migrants) of concern.
- Identify opportunities to maintain and/or increase connectivity across the landscape.

tain ungulates will be sensitive to climate change, but there is little evidence that their recent population trends are climate-driven.

As temperatures and precipitation patterns change over the coming decades, a better understanding of how climate change affects resources will become critical to effective mitigation and management. Climate change will interact with multiple stressors, such as land-use change, atmospheric pollution, and invasive species, many of which are more proximate than climate change, making it difficult to predict changes. The only certainty is that ecosystem properties, processes, and resources will continue to change over the next century. Species will be lost, others will

be gained, and disturbances will increase and alter the structure and function of ecosystems. Future management, monitoring, and research efforts will need to embrace these changing conditions.

Finally, through the synthesis process we were able to identify inventory, monitoring, and research needs that can lead to a better understanding of ecological responses to climate change in the Rocky Mountains and Upper Columbia Basin (Table 2). While these represent only a portion of the needs, our goal is to begin to guide future research directions and prioritization for the ROCO region.

Table 2. (continued)

Disturbance Regimes

Inventory & Monitoring
- Improve early detection of native and non-native invasive species and other exotic species.
- Improve region-wide assessment, maps, and spatial data on invasive presence and cover.
- Monitor sensitive habitats for invasive spread (e.g., high elevations, wetlands, and areas containing species of conservation concern).
- Monitor visitor use and other vectors of invasive spread (e.g., fishing and boating activity).
- Collect baseline monitoring information on native and non-native organisms.
- Increase collaboration and partnerships among federal, state, and private landowners to monitor disturbance and invasion across the West

Research
- Create bioclimatic models to predict the effect of climate change on invasive species ranges.
- Conduct research to discriminate between multiple climate variables' effects on disease.
- Develop forecast models for epidemics.
- Evaluate and understand the role of evolution in disease dynamics.

Alpine and Subalpine

Inventory & Monitoring
- Monitor long-term changes in alpine vegetation.
- Monitor native and exotic plant and animal migration upslope.

Research
- Research and monitor to document historical and future tree line movement in the mid- and southern Rockies through repeat photography and seedling establishment.
- Link changes in floras with fauna (e.g., plant community changes and pika/ptarmigan abundance).

Table 2. (continued)

Forests and Woodlands

Inventory & Monitoring
- Monitor aspen recruitment and growth following disturbance such as beetle-kill and fire.
- Monitor landscape-level changes in the character and distribution of forests through repeat photography and remote sensing.
- Develop better vegetation maps.
- Monitor the status and trends in forest growth and health.

Research
- Link local climate to vegetation.
- Research the feedbacks between insect, fire, and climate.
- Research and monitor forest recovery and wildlife use following widespread die-offs caused by insect infestations, blister rust, and fire.
- Understand the climate triggers for disturbance.
- Research the effects of climate change on mycorrhizae and their relationships with forest trees and other species with known fungal associations.
- Research the effects of microclimate on resistance of plant assemblages to climate change.

Sagebrush & Grasslands

Inventory & Monitoring
- Improve early invasive/exotic detection.
- Monitor the status and trends of invasive species.
- Monitor soil stability.
- Monitor status and trends of native and non-native vegetation.
- Monitor status and trends of important wildlife species such as sage grouse.

Research
- Examine the trends, causes, and consequences of woody encroachment.
- Research the multiple effects of grazing, climate, and fire on grasslands.

Aquatic Resources

Inventory & Monitoring
- Monitor the status and trends of wetlands.
- Continuously monitor streamflows and lake levels.
- Monitor status and trends in water quality.
- Monitor the status and trends of glaciers.
- Conduct wetlands inventories and vulnerability assessments.

Research
- Research changes in snowpack across elevational gradients.
- Research how warmer water temperatures and changing flows will affect aquatic organisms.
- Research high-elevation aquatic food webs and how they will be affected by climate change.
- Research the relationship between hydrology and wetland species composition and function.

Wildlife

Inventory & Monitoring
- Monitor status and trends in populations of at-risk species.
- Monitor status and trends in wildlife diseases and develop research linking disease outbreaks to climate change.

Research
- Research asynchronies in life history characters among interdependent species and the plasticity of species to adapt to disruptions.
- Research and monitor snow-dependent species.
- Research the effectiveness of different adaptation strategies for species of concern (e.g., nest boxes, food augmentation).
- Complete vulnerability assessments at large geographic scales and for land management units.
- Research the primary driver (e.g., temperature tolerances, precipitation changes vs. habitat/productivity response) of a species' response to climate change.

Chapter 8: Literature Cited

Abatzoglou, J. T., and K. T. Redmond. 2007. Asymmetry between trends in spring and autumn temperature and circulation regimes over western North America. Geophysical Research Letters 34:L18808.

Adams, R. A., and M. A. Hayes. 2008. Water availability and successful lactation by bats as related to climate change in arid regions of western North America. Journal of Animal Ecology 77:1115–1121.

Adler, P. B., J. HilleRisLambers, P. C. Kyriakidis, Q. Guan, and J. M. Levine. 2006. Climate variability has a stabilizing effect on the coexistence of prairie grasses. Proceedings of the National Academy of Sciences of the United States of America 103:12,793–12,798.

Aldridge, C. L., S. E. Nielsen, H. L. Beyer, M. S. Boyce, J. W. Connelly, S. T. Knick, and M. A. Schroeder. 2008. Range-wide patterns of greater sage-grouse persistence. Diversity and Distributions 14:983-994.

Allen, J. A., C. S. Brown, and T. J. Stohlgren. 2009. Non-native plant invasions of United States national parks. Biological Invasions 11:2195–2207.

Allen, C. D., A. K. Macalady, H. Chenchouni, D. Bachelet, N. McDowell, M. Vennetier, T. Kitzberger, A. Rigling, D. D. Breshears, E. H. Hogg, and others. 2010. A global overview of drought and heat-induced tree mortality reveals emerging climate change risks for forests. Forest Ecology and Management 259:660–684.

Anderson, L., C. E. Carlson, and R. H. Wakimoto. 1987. Forest fire frequency and western spruce budworm outbreaks in western Montana. Forest Ecology and Management 22:251–260.

Arno, S. F., and R. P. Hammerly. 1984. Timberline: Mountain and arctic forest frontiers. The Mountaineers, Seattle, Washington, USA.

Arno, S. F., and R. J. Hoff. 1990. Whitebark pine *Pinus albicaulis* Engelm. Pages 268–279 *in* R. M. Burns and B. H. Honkala, editors. Silvics of North America, Vol. 1, Conifers. USDA Forest Service, Agriculture Handbook. 654, Washington, D.C., USA.

Aw, J., and M. J. Kleeman. 2003. Evaluating the first-order effect of intraannual temperature variability on urban air pollution. Journal of Geophysical Research 108 (D12) Art. No. 4365.

Bachelet, D., J. Lenihan, R. Drapek, and R. Neilson. 2008. VEMAP vs VINCERA: A DGVM sensitivity to differences in climate scenarios. Global and Planetary Change 64:38–48.

Bachelet, D., R. P. Neilson, J. M. Lenihan, and R. J. Drapek. 2001. Climate change effects on vegetation distribution and carbon budget in the United States. Ecosystems 4:164–185.

Barnett, T. P., and D. W. Pierce. 2009. Sustainable water deliveries from the Colorado River in a changing climate. Proceedings of the National Academy of Sciences of the United States of America 106:7334-7338.

Barnett, T. P., D. W. Pierce, H. G. Hidalgo, C. Bonfils, B. D. Santer, T. Das, G. Bala, A. W. Wood, T. Nozawa, A. A. Mirin, D. R. Cayan, and M. D. Dettinger. 2008. Human-induced changes in the hydrology of the western United States. Science 319:1080–1083.

Baron, J. S. 2006. Hindcasting nitrogen deposition to determine an ecological critical load. Ecological Applications 16:433–439.

Baron, J. S., C. D. Allen, E. Fleishman, L. Gunderson, D. McKenzie, L. Meyerson, J. Oropeza, and N. Stephenson. 2008b. National Parks. Pages 4-1 to 4-68 *in* S. H. Julius and J. M. West, editors. Preliminary review of adaptation options for climate-sensitive ecosystems and resources. A Report by the US Climate Change Science Program and the Subcommittee on Global Change Research. US Environmental Protection Agency, Washington, D.C., USA.

Baron, J. S., M. D. Hartman, L. E. Band, and R. B. Lammers. 2000b. Sensitivity of a high-elevation rocky mountain watershed to altered climate and CO_2. Water Resources Research 36:89–99.

Baron, J. S., S. H. Julius, J. M. West, L. A. Joyce, G. M. Blate, C. H. Peterson, M. Palmer, B. D. Keller, P. Karieva, J. M. Scott, and B. Griffith. 2008a. Some guidelines for helping natural resources adapt to climate change. IHDP Update 2:46–52.

Baron, J. S., K. R. Nydick, H. M. Rueth, B. M.,Lafrancois, and A. P. Wolfe. 2003. High elevation ecosystem responses to atmospheric deposition of nitrogen in the Colorado Rocky Mountains, USA. Pages 429-436 *in* U. M. Huber, H. K. Bugmann, and M. A. Reasoner, editors. Global change and mountain regions: A state of knowledge overview. Kluwer Academic Publishers, Dordrecht, The Netherlands.

Baron, J. S., D. S. Ojima, E. A. Holland, and W. J. Parton. 1994. Analysis of nitrogen saturation potential in Rocky-Mountain tundra and forest—implications for aquatic systems. Biogeochemistry 27:61–82.

Baron, J. S., H. M. Rueth, A. M. Wolfe, K. R. Nydick, E. J. Allstott, J. T. Minear, and B. Moraska. 2000a. Ecosystem responses to nitrogen deposition in the Colorado Front Range. Ecosystems 3:352–368.

Baron, J. S., T. M. Schmidt, and M. D. Hartman. 2009. Climate-induced changes in high elevation stream nitrate dynamics. Global Change Biology 15:1777–1789.

Bartos, D. L. 2001. Landscape dynamics of aspen and conifer forests. USDA Forest Service Proceedings RMRS-P-18, Fort Collins, Colorado, USA.

Battin, J., M. W. Wiley, M. H. Ruckelshaus, R. N. Palmer, E. Korb, K. K. Bartz, and H. Imaki. 2007. Projected impacts of climate change on salmon habitat restoration. Proceedings of the National Academy of Sciences of the United States of America 104:6720–6725.

Beebee, T. J. C. 1995. Amphibian breeding and climate. Nature 374:219–220.

Beebee, T. J. C. 2002. Amphibian phenology and climate change. Conservation Biology 16:1454–1454.

Beever, E. A., P. F. Brussard, and J. Berger. 2003. Patterns of apparent extirpation among isolated populations of pikas (*Ochotona princeps*) in the Great Basin. Journal of Mammalogy 84:37–54.

Beever, E. A., C. Ray, P. W. Mote, and J. L. Wilkening. 2010. Testing alternative models of climate-mediated extirpations. Ecological Applications 20:164–178.

Bentz, B. 2008. Western US Bark Beetles and Climate Change. Available at http://www.fs.fed.us/ccrc/topics/bark-beetles.shtml. USDA Forest Service, Climate Change Resource Center.

Berger, J. 2004. The last mile: How to sustain long-distance migration in mammals. Conservation Biology 18:320–331.

Berger, J., S. L. Cain, and K. M. Berger. 2006. Connecting the dots: An invariant migration corridor links the Holocene to the present. Biology Letters 2:528-531.

Berlow, E. L., C. M. D'Antonio, and S. A. Reynolds. 2002. Shrub expansion in montane meadows: The interaction of local-scale disturbance and site aridity. Ecological Applications 12:1103–1118.

Bernard, S. M., J. M. Samet, A. Grambsch, K. L. Ebi, and I. Romieu. 2001. The potential impacts of climate variability and change on air pollution-related health effects in the United States. Environmental Health Perspectives 109:199–209.

Berthold P., Møller A.P. & Fiedler W. 2004. Page vii (Preface) in A. Møller, P. Berthold, and W. Fiedler, editors. Birds and climate change. Advances in Ecological Research 35. Elsevier Academic Press.

Binkley, D. 2008. Age distribution of aspen in Rocky Mountain National Park, USA. Forest Ecology and Management 255:797–802.

Birdnature. 1998. North American migration flyways. http://www.birdnature.com/flyways.html.

Blaustein, A.R., L.K. Belden, D. H. Olson, D.M. Green, T.L. Toot and J. M. Kiesecker. 2001. Amphibian breeding and climate change. Conservation Biology 15:1804–1809.

Blehert, D. S., A. C. Hicks, M. Behr, C. U. Meteyer, B. M. Berlowski-Zier, E. L. Buckles, J. T. H. Coleman, S. R. Darling, A. Gargas, R. Niver, J. C. Okoniewski, R. J. Rudd, and W. B. Stone. 2009. Bat white-nose syndrome: An emerging fungal pathogen? Science 323:227–227.

Blumenthal, D., R. A. Chimner, J. M. Welker, and J. A. Morgan. 2008. Increased snow facilitates plant invasion in mixedgrass prairie. New Phytologist 179:440–448.

Boisvenue, C., and S. W. Running. 2006. Impacts of climate change on natural forest productivity—evidence since the middle of the 20th century. Global Change Biology 12:862–882.

Bonfils, C., B. D. Santer, D. W. Pierce, H. G. Hidalgo, G. Bala, T. Das, T. P. Barnett, D. R. Cayan, C. Doutriaux, A. W. Wood, A. Mirin, and T. Nozawa. 2008. Detection and attribution of temperature changes in the mountainous western United States. Journal of Climate 21:6404-6424.

Bosch, J., L. M. Carrascal, L. Duran, S. Walker, and M. C. Fisher. 2007. Climate change and outbreaks of amphibian chytridiomycosis in a montane area of central Spain: Is there a link? Proceedings of the Royal Society B-Biological Sciences 274:253–260.

Both, C., S. Bouwhuis, C. M. Lessells, and M. E. Visser. 2006. Climate change and population declines in a long-distance migratory bird. Nature 441:81–83.

Bowman, W. D. 2000. Biotic controls over ecosystem response to environmental change in alpine tundra of the Rocky Mountains. Ambio 29:396–400.

Bowman, W. D. 2001. Introduction: Historical perspective and significance of alpine ecosystem studies. Pages 3–12 in W. D. Bowman and T. Seastedt, editors. Structure and function of an alpine ecosystem. Niwot Ridge, Colorado. Oxford University Press, New York, New York, USA.

Bowman, W. D., D. M. Cairns, J. S. Baron, and T. Seastedt. 2002. Islands in the sky: Alpine and treeline ecosystems of the Rockies. Pages 183–202 in J. S. Baron, editor. Rocky Mountain futures: An ecological perspective. Island Press, Washington, D.C., USA.

Bowman, W., J. Larson, K. Holland, M. Wiedermann, and J. Nieves. 2006. Nitrogen critical loads for alpine vegetation and terrestrial ecosystem response—Are we there yet? Ecological Applications 16:1183–1193.

Bradley, B. A. 2010. Assessing ecosystem threats from global and regional change: Hierarchical modeling of risk to sagebrush ecosystems from climate change, land use and invasive species in Nevada, USA. Ecography 33:198–208.

Bradley, B. A., M. Oppenheimer, and D. S. Wilcove. 2009. Climate change and plant invasions: Restoration opportunities ahead? Global Change Biology 15:1511–1521.

Bradshaw, W. E., and C. M. Holzapfel. 2006. Evolutionary response to rapid climate change. Science 312:1477–1478.

Brazda, A. R. 1953. Elk migration patterns, and some of the factors affecting movements in the Gallatin River drainage, Montana. Journal of Wildlife Management 17:9–23.

Breshears, D. D., N. S. Cobb, P. M. Rich, K. P. Price, C. D. Allen, R. G. Balice, W. H. Romme, J. H. Kastens, M. L. Floyd, J. Belnap, J. J. Anderson, O. B. Myers, and C. W. Meyer. 2005. Regional vegetation die-off in response to global-change-type drought. Proceedings of the National Academy of Sciences of the United States of America 102:15,144-15,148.

Britten, M., E. W. Schweiger, B. Frakes, D. Manier, and D. Pillmore. 2007. Rocky Mountain Network vital signs monitoring plan. Natural Resource Report NPS/ROMN/ NRR-2007/010.

Brown, T. J., B. L. Hall, and A. L. Westerling. 2004. The impact of twenty-first century climate change on wildland fire danger in the western United States: An applications perspective. . Climatic Change 62:365–388.

Bunting, S. C., J. L. Kingery, M. A. Hemstrom, M. A. Schroeder, R. A. Gravenmier, and W. J. Hann. 2002. Altered rangeland ecosystems in the Interior Columbia Basin. General Technical Report PNW-GTR-553. USDA Forest Service, Pacific Northwest Research Station, Portland, Oregon, USA.

Burkett, V., and J. Kusler. 2000. Climate change: Potential impacts and interactions in wetlands of the United States. Journal of the American Water Resources Association 36:313–320.

Burns, C. E., K. M. Johnston, and O. J. Schmitz. 2003. Global climate change and mammalian species diversity in US national parks. Proceedings of the National Academy of Sciences of the United States of America 100:11474–11477.

Butler, D. R., G. P. Malanson, and D. M. Cairns. 1994. Stability of alpine treeline in northern Montana, USA. Phytocoenologia 22:485–500.

Carey, C. 2000. Infectious disease and worldwide declines of amphibiain populations, with comments on emerging diseases in coral reef organisms and in humans. Environmental Health Perspectives, Supplement 108(1):143–150.

Carey, C., and M. A. Alexander. 2003. Climate change and amphibian declines: Is there a link? Diversity and Distributions 9:111–121.

Cayan, D. R., S. A. Kammerdiener, M. D. Dettinger, J. Caprio, and D. H. Peterson. 2001. Changes in the onset of spring in the western United States. Bulletin of the American Meteorological Society 82:399–415.

Chambers, J. C., B. A. Roundy, R. R. Blank, S. E. Meyer, and A. Whittaker. 2007. What makes Great Basin sagebrush ecosystems invasible by *Bromus tectorum*? Ecological Monographs 77:117–145.

Chambers, J. C., and M. J. Wisdom. 2009. Priority research and management issues for the imperiled Great Basin of the western United States. Restoration Ecology 17:707–714.

Ciarniello, L. M., M. S. Boyce, D. R. Seip, and D. C. Heard. 2009. Comparison of grizzly bear *Ursus arctos* demographics in wilderness mountains versus a plateau with resource development. Wildlife Biology 15:247–265.

CIG [Climate Impacts Group]. 2010. http://cses.washington.edu/cig/. University of Washington, Seattle, Washington, USA.

Civerolo, K. L., C. Hogrefe, B. Lynn, C. Rosenzweig, R. Goldberg, J. Rosenthal, K. Knowlton, and P. L. Kinney. 2008. Simulated effects of climate change on summertime nitrogen deposition in the eastern US. Atmospheric Environment 42:2074–2082.

Cleland, E. E., N. R. Chiariello, S. R. Loarie, H. A. Mooney, and C. B. Field. 2006. Diverse responses of phenology to global changes in a grassland ecosystem. Proceedings of the National Academy of Sciences of the United States of America 103:13740–13744.

CoDoW [Colorado Department of Wildlife]. 2009. Threatened and Endangered List. Online. http://wildlife.state.co.us/WildlifeSpecies/SpeciesOfConcern/ThreatenedEndangeredList/ListOfThreatenedAndEndangeredSpecies.htm. Accessed 10 June 2010.

Collins, B., J. Miller, A. Thode, M. Kelly, J. van Wagtendonk, and S. Stephens. 2009. Interactions among wildland fires in a long-established Sierra Nevada natural fire area. ecosystems 12:114–128.

Cook, E. R., R. Seager, M. A. Cane, and D. W. Stahle. 2007. North American drought: Reconstructions, causes, and consequences. Earth Science Reviews 81:93–134.

Cook, E. R., C. A. Woodhouse, C. M. Eakin, D. M. Meko, and D. W. Stahle. 2004. Long-term aridity changes in the western United States. Science 306:1015–1018.

Copeland, H. E., K. E. Doherty, D. E. Naugle, A. Pocewicz, and J. M. Kiesecker. 2009. Mapping oil and gas development potential in the US intermountain west and estimating impacts to species. PLoS ONE 4(10):e7400.

Copeland, J. P., K. S. McKelvey, K. B. Aubry, A. Landa, J. Persson, R. M. Inman, J. Krebs, E. Lofroth, H. Golden, J. R. Squires, A. Magoun, M. K. Schwartz, J. Wilmot, C. L. Copeland, R. E. Yates, I. Kojola, and R. May. 2010. The bioclimatic envelope of the wolverine (*Gulo gulo*): Do climatic constraints limits its geographic distribution? Canadian Journal of Zoology 88:233–246.

Corn, P. S. 2003. Amphibian breeding and climate change: Importance of snow in the mountains. Conservation Biology 17:622–625.

Corn, P. S. 2005. Climate change and amphibians. Animal biodiversity and conservation 28:59-67.

Corn, P. S., and E. Muths. 2002. Variable breeding phenology affects the exposure of amphibian embryos to ultraviolet radiation. Ecology 83:2958–2963.

Cox, G. 1999. Alien species in North America and Hawaii: Impacts on natural ecosystems. Island Press, Washington D.C., USA.

Crozier, L. 2003. Winter warming facilitates range expansion: Cold tolerance of the butterfly Atalopedes campestris. Oecologia 135:648–656.

Crozier, L. 2004. Warmer winters drive butterfly range expansion by increasing survivorship. Ecology 85:231–241.

Cryan, P. M. 2003. Seasonal distribution of migratory tree bats (Lasiurus and Lasionycteris) in North America. Journal of Mammalogy 84:579–593.

Cryan, P. M., M. A. Bogan, and J. S. Altenbach. 2000. Effect of elevation on distribution of female bats in the Black Hills, South Dakota. Journal of Mammalogy 81:719–725.

Cryan, P. M., and A. C. Brown. 2007. Migration of bats past a remote island offers clues toward the problem of bat fatalities at wind turbines. Biological Conservation 139:1–11.

Creel, S., and M. Creel. 2009. Density-dependence and climate effects in Rocky Mountain elk: An application of regression with instrumental variables for population time series with sampling error. Journal of Animal Ecology 78:1291–1297.

Crick, H. Q. P., C. Dudley, D. E. Glue, and D. L. Thomson. 1997. UK birds are laying their eggs earlier. Nature 388:526

Cross, P. C., E. K. Cole, A. P. Dobson, W. H. Edwards, K. L. Hamlin, G. Luikart, A. D. Middleton, B. M. Scurlock, and P. J. White. 2010. Probable causes of increasing brucellosis in free-ranging elk of the Greater Yellowstone Ecosystem. Ecological Applications 20:278–288.

Cross, M. S., J. A. Hilty, G. M. Tabor, J. J. Lawler, L. J. Graumlich, and J. Berger. From connect-the-dots to dynamic networks: Maintaining and enhancing connectivity as a strategy to address climate change impacts on wildlife. *In* J. Brodie, E. Post, and D. Doak, editors. Wildlife conservation in a changing climate. Chicago University Press, Chicago, Illinois, USA, in press.

Crutzen, P. J., and J. G. Goldhammer, editors. 1993. Fire in the environment: The ecological, atmospheric, and climatic importance of vegetation fires. Wiley, New York, New York, USA.

Currano, E. D., P. Wilf, S. L. Wing, C. C. Labandeira, E. C. Lovelock, and D. L. Royer. 2008. Sharply increased insect herbivory during the Paleocene–Eocene Thermal Maximum. Proceedings of the National Academy of Sciences of the United States of America 105:1960–1964.

Dale, V. H., L. A. Joyce, S. McNulty, R. P. Neilson, M. P. Ayres, M. D. Flannigan, P. J. Hanson, L. C. Irland, A. E. Lugo, C. J. Peterson, D. Simberloff, F. J. Swanson, B. J. Stocks, and B. M. Wotton. 2001. Climate change and forest disturbances. BioScience 51:723–734.

D'Antonio, C. M., and P. M. Vitousek. 2003. Biological invasions by exotic grasses, the grass/fire cycle, and global change. Annual Review of Ecology and Systematics 23:63–87.

Daszak, P. L. Berger, A. Cunningham, A. Hyatt, D. Green, and R. Speare. 1999. Emerging infectious diseases and amphibian population declines. Emerging Infectious Diseases 5:735–748.

De Valpine, P., and J. Harte. 2001. Plant responses to experimental warming in a montane meadow. Ecology 82:637–648.

DeByle, N. V., and R. P. Winokur. 1985. Aspen: Ecology and management in the western United States. General Technical Report RM-119. USDA Forest Service, Rocky Mountain Forest and Range Experiment Station, Fort Collins, Colorado, USA.

DEFRA [Department of Environment, Food and Rural Affairs]. 2005. Climate change and migratory species. A report by the British Trust for Ornithology. http://www.defra.gov.uk/wildlife-countryside/resprog/findings/climatechange-migratory/index.htm.

Diaz, H. F., and J. K. Eischeid. 2007. Disappearing "alpine tundra" Köppen climatic type in the western United States. Geophysical Research Letters 34:L18707.

Dobkin, D. S., R. D. Gettinger, and M. G. Gerdes. 1995. Springtime movements, roost use, and foraging activity of Townsend big-eared bat (*Plecotis townsendii*) in central Oregon. Great Basin Naturalist 55:315–321.

Dodd, C.K., Jr., and L. L. Smith. 2003. Habitat destruction and alteration. Historical trends and future prospects for amphibians. Pages 94–112 *in* R.D. Semlitsch, editor. Amphibian Conservation. Smithsonian Institution Press, Washington, D.C., USA.

Donnelly, M.A., and M.L. Crump. 1998. Potential effects of climate change on two neotropical amphibian assemblages. Climate Change 39:541–561.

Dukes, J. S., and H. A. Mooney. 1999. Does global change increase the success of biological invaders? Trends in Ecology & Evolution 14:135–139.

Dunn, P.O., and D.W.Winkler. 1999. Climate change has affected the breeding date of tree swallows throughout North America. Proceedings of the Royal Society of London 266:2487–2490.

Ehrenfeld, J. G. 2003. Effects of exotic plant invasions on soil nutrient cycling processes. Ecosystems 6:503–523.

Elliott, G. P., and W. L. Baker. 2004. Quaking aspen (*Populus tremuloides* Michx.) at treeline: A century of change in the San Juan Mountains, Colorado, USA. Journal of Biogeography 31:733–745.

Fagre, D. B. 2009. Introduction: Understanding the importance of alpine treeline ecotones in mountain ecosystems. Pages 1–10 *in* D. R. Butler, G. P. Malanson, S. J. Walsh, and D. B. Fagre, editors. The changing alpine treeline. Elsevier, Netherlands.

Fahrig L. 2002. Effect of habitat fragmentation on the extinction threshold: A synthesis. Ecological Applications 12:346–353.

Fang, X., and H. G. Stefan. 1998. Potential climate warming effects on ice covers of small lakes in the contiguous US Cold Regions Science and Technology 27:119–140.

Fang, X., and H. G. Stefan. 1999. Projections of climate change effects on water temperature characteristics of small lakes in the contiguous US. Climatic Change 42:377–412.

Fausch, K. D., Y. Taniguchi, S. Nakano, G. D. Grossman, and C. R. Townsend. 2001. Flood disturbance regimes influence rainbow trout invasion success among five holartic regions. Ecological Applications 11:1438–1455.

Fenn, M. E., J. S. Baron, E. B. Allen, H. M. Rueth, K. R. Nydick, L. Geiser, W. D. Bowman, J. O. Sickman, T. Meixner, D. W. Johnson, and P. Neitlich. 2003. Ecological effects of nitrogen deposition in the western United States. BioScience 53:404–420.

Ficetola, G. F., W. Thuiller, and C. Miaud. 2007. Prediction and validation of the potential global distribution of a problematic alien invasive species - the American bullfrog. Diversity and Distributions 13:476-485.

Fiedler, W. 2003. Recent changes in migratory behavior of birds: A compilation of field observations and ringing data. Pages 21-38 *in* P. Berthold, E. Gwinner, and E. Sonnenschein, editors. Avian migration. Springer Verlag, Berlin.

Fiedler, W. 2009. Bird ecology as an indicator of climate and global change. Pages 181-196 *in* T. M. Letcher, editor. Climate change: Observed impacts on planet Earth. Elsevier, Amsterdam.

Field, C. B., L. D. Mortsch, M. Brklacich, D. L. Forbes, P. Kovacs, J. A. Patz, S. W. Running, and M. J. Scott. 2007. North America: Contribution of working group II to the fourth assessment report of the Intergovernmental Panel on Climate Change. Pages 617–652 *in* M. L. Parry, O. F. Canziani, J. P. Palutikof, P. J. van der Linden, and C. E. Hanson, editors. Climate change 2007: Impacts, adaptation and vulnerability. Cambridge University Press, Cambridge, UK.

Flannigan, M., B. Amiro, K. Logan, B. Stocks, and B. Wotton. 2006. Forest fires and climate change in the 21st Century. Mitigation and Adaptation Strategies for Global Change 11:847–859.

Forister, M. L., A. C. McCall, N. J. Sanders, J. A. Fordyce, J. H. Thorne, J. O'Brien, D. P. Waetjen, and A. M. Shapiro. 2010. Compounded effects of climate change and habitat alteration shift patterns of butterfly diversity. Proceedings of the National Academy of Sciences of the United States of America 107:2088–2092.

Fountain, A. 2006. Glaciers of the American West. Available at http://glaciers.research.pdx.edu/states.php. Portland State University, Portland, Washington, USA.

Frank, D. A. 2007. Drought effects on above- and belowground production of a grazed temperate grassland ecosystem. Oecologia 152:131–139.

Frank, D. A., and S. J. McNaughton. 1993. Evidence for the promotion of aboveground grassland production by native large herbivores in Yellowstone National Park. Oecologia 96:157–161.

Frankel, S. J. 2008. Forest plant disease and climate change. Available at http://www.fs.fed.us/ccrc/topics/plant-diseases.shtml. USDA Forest Service, Climate Change Resource Center.

Galatowitsch, S., L. Frelich, and L. Phillips-Mao. 2009. Regional climate change adaptation strategies for biodiversity conservation in a midcontinental region of North America. Biological Conservation 142:2012–2022.

Galbreath, K. E., D. J. Hafner, and K. R. Zamudio. 2009. When cold is better: Climate-driven elevation shifts yield complex patterns of diversification and demography in an alpine specialist (American pika, Ochotona princeps). Evolution 63:2848–2863.

Galloway, J. N., J. D. Aber, J. W. Erisman, S. P. Seitzinger, R. W. Howarth, E. B. Cowling, and B. J. Cosby. 2003. The nitrogen cascade. Bioscience 53:341–356.

GAO [Government Accountability Office]. 2007. Climate change: Agencies should develop guidance for addressing the effects on federal land and water resources. GAO-07-863. Washington. D.C., USA.

Garrett, L. K., T. J. Rodhouse, G. H. Dicus, C. C. Caudill, and M. R. Shardlow. 2007. Upper Columbia Basin Network vital signs monitoring plan.. Natural Resource Report NPS/UCBN/NRR-2007/002. National Park Service, Fort Collins, Colorado, USA.

Gibbons, J. W. and D. H. Bennett. 1974. Determination of anuran terrestrial activity patterns by a drift fence method. Copeia 1974:236–243.

Gonzales, P., R.P. Neilson, K.S. McKelvey, J.M. Lenihan, and R.J. Drapek. 2007. Potential impacts of climate change on habitat and conservation priority areas for Lynx canadensis (Canada lynx). Report to the Forest Service, US Department of Agriculture, Washington D.C., and NatureServe, Arlington, Virginia, USA.

Gooseff, M. N., K. Strzepek, and S. C. Chapra. 2005. Modeling the potential effects of climate change on water temperature downstream of a shallow reservoir, Lower Madison River, MT. Climatic Change 68:331–353.

Gough, L., C. W. Osenberg, K. L. Gross, and S. L. Collins. 2000. Fertilization effects on species density and primary productivity in herbaceous plant communities. Oikos 89:428–439.

Grabherr, G., M. Gottfried, and H. Pauli. 1994. Climate effects on mountain plants. Nature 369:448–448.

Graumlich, L. J., L. A. Waggoner, and A. G. Bunn. 2005. Detecting global change at alpine treeline: Coupling paleoecology with contemporary studies. Pages 501–508 *in* U. M. Huber, H. Bugmann, and M. A. Reasoner, editors. Global change and mountain regions: An overview of current knowledge. Springer, Netherlands.

Gray, D. 2008. The relationship between climate and outbreak characteristics of the spruce budworm in eastern Canada. Climatic Change 87:361–383.

Groot, C., and L. Margolis. 1991. Pacific salmon life histories. UBC Press, Vancouver, British Columbia, Canada.

Guenther, A. 2002. The contribution of reactive carbon emissions from vegetation to the carbon balance of terrestrial ecosystems. Chemosphere 49:837–844.

Guralnick, R. 2006. The legacy of past climate and landscape change on species' current experienced climate and elevation ranges across latitude: A multispecies study utilizing mammals in western North America. Global Ecology and Biogeography 15:505–518.

Gurevitch, J., and D. K. Padilla. 2004. Are invasive species a major cause of extinctions? Trends in Ecology & Evolution 19:470–474.

Hafner, D. J., and R. M. Sullivan. 1995. Historical and ecological biogeography of nearctic pikas (Lagomorpha, Ochotonidae). Journal of Mammalogy 76:302–321.

Hall, M. H. P., and D. B. Fagre. 2003. Modeled climate-induced glacier change in Glacier National Park, 1850–2100. BioScience 53:131–140.

Hamlet, A. F., and D. P. Lettenmaier. 2007. Effects of 20th century warming and climate variability on flood risk in the western US Water Resources. Research 43:W06427.

Hamlet, A. F., P. W. Mote, M. P. Clark, and D. P. Lettenmaier. 2005. Effects of temperature and precipitation variability on snowpack trends in the western United States. Journal of Climate 18:4545-4561.

Hamlet, A. F., P. W. Mote, M. P. Clark, and D. P. Lettenmaier. 2007. Twentieth-century trends in runoff, evapotranspiration, and soil moisture in the western United States. Journal of Climate 20:1468–1486.

Hamrick, J. L. 2004. Response of forest trees to global environmental changes. Forest Ecology and Management 197:323–335.

Hansen, A. J., R. A. Y. Rasker, B. Maxwell, J. J. Rotella, J. D. Johnson, A. W. Parmenter, U. T. E. Langner, W. B. Cohen, R. L. Lawrence, and M. P. V. Kraska. 2009. Ecological causes and consequences of demographic change in the new west. BioScience 52:151–162.

Hari, R. E., D. M. Livingstone, R. Siber, P. Burkhardt-Holm, and H. Guttinger. 2006. Consequences of climatic change for water temperature and brown trout populations in Alpine rivers and streams. Global Change Biology 12:10–26.

Haroldson, M. A., M. Ternent, K. A. Gunther, and C. C. Schwartz. 2002. Grizzly bear denning chronology and movements in the Greater Yellowstone Ecosystem. *Ursus* 13:29–37.

Harper, M. P., and B. L. Peckarsky. 2006. Emergence cues of a mayfly in a high-altitude stream ecosystem: Potential response to climate change. Ecological Applications 16:612–621.

Hart, J. H., and D. L. Hart. 2001. Interaction among cervids, fungi, and aspen in northwest Wyoming. Pages 197–205 in W. Sheppard, D. D. Binkley, D. L. Bartos, T. J. Stohlgren, L. G. Eskew, compilers. Proceedings RMRS-P-18. USDA Forest Service, Rocky Mountain Research Station, Fort Collins, Colorado, USA..

Harte, J., and R. Shaw. 1995. Shifting dominance within a montane vegetation community: Results of a climate-warming experiment. Science 267:876–880.

Harvell, C. D., C. E. Mitchell, J. R. Ward, S. Altizer, A. P. Dobson, R. S. Ostfeld, and M. D. Samuel. 2002. Climate warming and disease risks for terrestrial and marine biota. Science 296:2158–2162.

Harvey, A. E., J. W. Byler, G. I. McDonald, L. F. Neuenschwander, and J. R. Tonn. 2008. Death of an ecosystem: Perspectives on western white pine ecosystems of North America at the end of the twentieth century. General Technical Report RMRS-GTR-208. USDA Forest Service, Rocky Mountain Research Station, Fort Collins, Colorado, USA.

Hauer, F. R., J. S. Baron, D. Campbell, K. D. Fausch, S. Hostetler, W., G. H. Leavesley, P. R. Leavitt, D. McKnight, and J. A. Stanford. 1997. Assessment of climate change and freshwater ecosystems of the Rocky Mountains, USA and Canada. Hydrological Processes 11:903–924.

Hayes, M. P., and M. R. Jennings. 1986. Decline of ranid frog species in western North America—Are bullfrogs (*Rana catesbeiana*) responsible? Journal of Herpetology 20:490–509.

Hellmann, J. J., J. E. Byers, B. G. Bierwagen, and J. S. Dukes. 2008. Five potential consequences of climate change for invasive species. Conservation Biology 22:534–543.

Hessl, A. 2002. Aspen, elk, and fire: The effects of human institutions on ecosystem processes. BioScience 52:1011–1022.

Hessl, A. E., and W. L. Baker. 1997. Spruce and fir regeneration and climate in the forest-tundra ecotone of Rocky Mountain National Park, Colorado USA. Arctic and Alpine Research 29:173–183.

Hessl, A. E., D. McKenzie, and R. Schellhaas. 2004. Drought and Pacific Decadl Oscillation linked to fire occurrence in the inland Pacific northwest. Ecological Applications 14:425–442.

Hickling, R., D. B. Roy, J. K. Hill, and C. D. Thomas. 2005. A northward shift of range margins in British Odonata. Global Change Biology 11:502–506.

Higgins, P. A. T., and J. Harte. 2006. Biophysical and Biogeochemical Responses to Climate Change Depend on Dispersal and Migration. BioScience 56:407-417.

Higgins, S. I., and Richardson D. M. 1999. Predicting plant migration rates in a changing world: The role of long-distance dispersal. American Naturalist 153:464–475.

Hitch, A. T., and P. L Leberg. 2007. Breeding distributions of North American birds species moving north as a result of climate change. Conservation Biology 21:534–539.

Hogg, I. D., and D. D. Williams. 1996. Response of stream invertebrates to a global-warming thermal regime: An ecosystem-level manipulation. ecology 77:395–407.

Hoskinson, R. L., and J. R. Tester. 1980. Migration behavior of pronghorn in southeastern Idaho. Journal of Wildlife Management 44:132–144.

Hostetler, S. W., and E. E. Small. 1999. Response of North American freshwater lakes to simulated future climates. Journal of the American Water Resources Association 35:1625–1637.

Humphries, M. M., D. W. Thomas, and J. R. Speakman. 2002. Climate-mediated energetic constraints on the distribution of hibernating mammals. Nature 418:313–316.

Hutchison, V. H, and R. K. Dupré. 1992. Thermoregulation. Pages 206–249 *in* M. E. Feder, W. W. Burggren, editors. Environmental physiology of the amphibians. University of Chicago Press, Chicago, Illinois, USA.

IDFG [Idaho Department of Fish and Game]. 2009. Idaho comprehensive wildlife conservation strategy. Online. http://fishandgame.idaho.gov/cdc/cwcs_table_of_contents.cfm. Accessed 10 June 2010.

Ingersoll, G. P., M. A. Mast, D. H. Campbell, D. W. Clow, L. Nanus, and J. T. Turk. 2008. Trends in snowpack chemistry and comparison to National Atmospheric Deposition Program results for the Rocky Mountains, US, 1993–2004. Atmospheric Environment 42:6098–6113.

Inkley, D. B., M. G. Anderson, A. R. Blaustein, V. R. Burkett, B. Felzer, B. Griffith, J. Price, and T. L. Root. 2004. Global climate change and wildlife in North America. Wildlife Society Technical Review 04–2. The Wildlife Society, Bethesda, Maryland, USA.

Inouye, D. W. 2008. Effects of climate change on phenology, frost damage, and floral abundance of montane wildflowers. Ecology 89:353–362.

Inouye, D. W., B. Barr, K. B. Armitage, and B. D. Inouye. 2000. Climate change is affecting altitudinal migrants and hibernating species. Proceedings of the National Academy of Sciences of the United States of America 97:1630–1633.

Izaurralde, R. C., A. M. Thomson, N. J. Rosenberg, and R. A. Brown. 2005. Climate change impacts for the conterminous USA: An integrated assessment. Part 6. Distribution and productivity of unmanaged ecosystems. Climatic Change 69:107–126.

Jacob, D. J., and D. A. Winner. 2009. Effect of climate change on air quality. Atmospheric Environment 43:51–63.

Jacques, C. N., J. A. Jenks, and R. W. Klaver. 2009. Seasonal movements and home-range use by female pronghorns in sagebrush-steppe communities of western South Dakota. Journal of Mammalogy 90:433-441.

Janetos, A., L. Hansen, D. Inouye, B .P. Kelly, L. Meyerson, B. Peterson, and R. Shaw. 2008. Biodiversity. Chapter 5 in The Effects of Climate Change on Agriculture, Land Resources, Water Resources, and Biodiversity in the United States. US Climate Change Science Program, Washington, D.C., USA..

Jean, C., A. Schrag, R. Bennetts, R. Daley, E. Crowe, and S. O'Ney. 2005. Vital signs monitoring plan for the Greater Yellowstone Network. . National Park Service, Greater Yellowstone Network, Bozeman, Montana, USA.

Jones, T., and W. Cresswell. 2010. The phenology mismatch hypothesis: Are declines of migrant birds linked to uneven global climate change? Journal of Animal Ecology 79:98–108.

Joyce, L. A., G. M. Blate, S. G. McNulty, C. I. Millar, S. Moser, R. P. Neilson, and D. L. Peterson. 2009. Managing for multiple resources under climate change: National forests. Environmental Management 44:1022–1032.

Joyce, L. A., C. H. Flather, and M. Koopman. 2008. Analysis of potential impacts of climate change on wildlife habitats in the US 10-31-08 Final Report, Wildlife Habitat Policy Research Program. USDA Forest Service. Rocky Mountain Research Station, Fort Collins, Colorado, USA.

Karl, T., J. Melillo, and T. Peterson, editors. 2009. Global climate change impacts in the United States. Cambridge University Press, Cambridge, England.

Karnosky, D. F., K. S. Pregitzer, D. R. Zak, M. E. Kubiske, G. R. Hendrey, D. Weinstein, M. Nosal, and K. E. Percy. 2005. Scaling ozone responses of forest trees to the ecosystem level in a changing climate. Plant Cell and Environment 28:965–981.

Kashian, D. M., W. H. Romme, and C. M. Regan. 2007. Reconciling divergent interpretations of quaking aspen decline on the northern Colorado Front Range. Ecological Applications 17:1296–1311.

Kaye, M. W., D. Binkley, and T. J. Stohlgren. 2005. Effects of conifers and elk browsing on quaking aspen forests in the central Rocky Mountains, USA. Ecological Applications 15:1284–1295.

Keane, R. E., and S. F. Arno. 1993. Rapid decline of whitebark pine in western Montana: Evidence from 20-year remeasurements. Western Journal of Applied Forestry 8:44–47.

Keane, R. E., K. C. Ryan, T. T. Veblen, C. D. Allen, J. Logan, and B. Hawkes. 2002. The cascading effects of fire exclusion in Rocky Mountain ecosystems. Pages 133–152 in J. S. Baron, editor. Rocky Mountain futures: An ecological perspective. Island Press, Washington, D.C., USA.

Keleher, C. J., and F. J. Rahel. 1996. Thermal limits to salmonid distributions in the rocky mountain region and potential habitat loss due to global warming: A geographic information system (GIS) approach. Transactions of the American Fisheries Society 125:1-13.

Kelsey, R. G., and G. Joseph. 2003. Ethanol in ponderosa pine as an indicator of physiological injury from fire and its relationship to secondary beetles. Canadian Journal Of Forest Research 33:870–884.

Kendall, K.C. 2010. Whitebark pine communities. http://www.nrmsc.usgs.gov/research/whitebar.htm. Accessed 10 June 2010.

Kendall, K. C., D. Ayers, and D. Schirokauer. 1996. Limber pine status from Alberta to Wyoming. Nutcracker Notes 7:23–24.

Kendall, K. C., and R. E. Keane. 2001. Whitebark pine decline: Infection, mortality, and population trends. Pages 221–242 in D. F. Tomback, S. F. Arno, and R. E. Keane, editors. Whitebark pine communities: Ecology and restoration. Island Press, Washington, D.C., USA.

Kendall, K. C., J. B. Stetz, J. Boulanger, A. C. Macleod, D. Paetkau, and G. C. White. 2009. Demography and genetic structure of a recovering grizzly bear population. Journal of Wildlife Management 73:3–17.

Kendall, K. C., J. B. Stetz, D. A. Roon, L. P. Waits, J. B. Boulanger, and D. Paetkau. 2008. Grizzly bear density in Glacier National Park, Montana. Journal of Wildlife Management 72:1693–1705.

Kiesecker, J. M., and A. R. Blaustein. 1995. Synergism between UV-B radiation and a pathogen magnifies amphibian embryo mortality in nature. Proceedings of the National Academy of Sciences of the United States of America 92:11049–11052.

Kiesecker, J. M., A. R. Blaustein, and L. K. Belden. 2001. Complex causes of amphibian population declines. Nature 410:681–684.

Kitzberger, T., P.M. Brown, E.K. Heyerdahl, T.W. Swetnam, and T.T. Veblen (2007). Contingent Pacific-Atlantic Ocean influence on multi-century wildfire synchrony over western North America. Proceedings of the National Academy of Sciences of the United States of America 104:543-548.

Kittel, T. G. F., P. E. Thornton, A. Royle, and T. N. Chase. 2002. Climates of the Rocky Mountains: Historical and future patterns. Pages 59–82 in J. S. Baron, editor. Rocky Mountain futures: An ecological perspective. Island Press, Washington, D.C., USA.

Klasner, F. L., and D. B. Fagre. 2002. A half century of change in alpine treeline patterns at Glacier National Park, Montana, USA. Arctic Antarctic and Alpine Research 34:49–56.

Knapp, P. A. 1998. Spatio-temporal patterns of large grassland fires in the Intermountain West, USA. Global Ecology and Biogeography Letters 7:259–272.

Knapp, A. K., P. A. Fay, J. M. Blair, S. L. Collins, M. D. Smith, J. D. Carlisle, C. W. Harper, B. T. Danner, M. S. Lett, and J. K. McCarron. 2002. Rainfall variability, carbon cycling, and plant species diversity in a mesic grassland. Science 298:2202–2205.

Knick, S. T., D. S. Dobkin, J. T. Rotenberry, M. A. Schroeder, W. M. Vander Haegen, and C. van Riper. 2003. Teetering on the edge or too late? Conservation and research issues for avifauna of sagebrush habitats. Condor 105:611–634.

Knick, S. T., A. L. Holmes and R. F. Miller. 2005. The role of fire in structuring sagebrush habitats and bird communities. Studies in Avian Biology 30:63–75.

Knick, S. T., and J. T. Rotenberry. 2000. Ghosts of habitats past: Contribution of landscape change to current habitats used by shrubland birds. Ecology 81:220-227.

Knowles, N., M. D. Dettinger, and D. R. Cayan. 2006. Trends in snowfall versus rainfall in the western United States. Journal of Climate 18:4,545–544,559.

Konrad, C. P., and D. B. Booth. 2005. Ecological significance of hydrologic changes in

urban streams. Pages 157–177 in L. R. Brown, R. H. Gray, R. M. Hughes, and M. R. Meador, editors. Effects of urbanization on stream ecosystems. American Fisheries Society, Symposium 47, Bethesda, Maryland, USA.

Koteen L. 1999. Climate change, whitebark pine, and grizzly bears in the Greater Yellowstone Ecosystem. M.S. Thesis. School of Forestry and Environmental Studies, Yale University, New Haven, Connecticut.

Kreuzer, M. P., and N. J. Huntly. 2003. Habitat-specific demography: Evidence for source-sink population structure in a mammal, the pika. Oecologia 134:343–349.

Kruse, C. G., W. Hurbert, and F. J. Rahel. 1997. Geomorphic influences on the distribution of Yellowstone cutthroat trout in the Absaroka Mountains, Wyoming. Transactions of the American Fisheries Society 126:418–427.

Kulakowski, D., T. T. Veblen, and B. P. Kurzel. 2006. Influences of infrequent fire, elevation and pre-fire vegetation on the persistence of quaking aspen (Populus tremuloides Michx.) in the Flat Tops area, Colorado, USA. Journal of Biogeography 33:1397–1413.

Kumar, S., S. A. Spaulding, T. J. Stohlgren, K. A. Hermann, T. S. Schmidt, and L. L. Bahls. 2009. Potential habitat distribution for the freshwater diatom Didymosphenia geminata in the continental US. Frontiers in Ecology and the Environment 7:415–420.

Kusler, J. 2006. Common questions: Wetlands, climate change, and carbon sequestering. . Association of State Wetland Managers, Berne, New York, USA.

La Sorte, F. A., and W. Jetz. 2010. Avian distributions under climate change: Towards improved projections. Journal of Experimental Biology 213:862–869.

La Sorte, F. A., and F. R. Thompson. 2007. Poleward shifts in winter ranges of North American birds. Ecology 88:1803–812.

Landers, D. H., S. L. Simonich, D. A. Jaffe, L. H. Geiser, D. H. Campbell, A. R. Schwindt, C. B. Schreck, M. L. Kent, W. D. Hafner, H. E. Taylor, K. J. Hageman, S. Usenko, L. K., Ackerman, J. E. Schrlau, N. . Rose, T. F. Blett, and M. M. Erway. 2008. The fate, transport, and ecological impacts of airborne contaminants in western national parks (USA). EPA/600/R-07/138. US Environmental Protection Agency, Office of Research and Development, NHEERL, Western Ecology Division, Corvallis, Oregon, USA.

Landhausser, S. M., D. Deshaies, and V. J. Lieffers. 2010. Disturbance facilitates rapid range expansion of aspen into higher elevations of the Rocky Mountains under a warming climate. Journal of Biogeography 37:68–76.

Lawler, J. J., S. I. Shafer, B. A. Bancroft and A.R. Blaustein. 2009. Projected climate impacts for amphibians of the Western Hemisphere. Conservation Biology 24:38–50.

Lawler, J.J., S.I. Shafer, D. White, P. Kareiva, E. P. Maurer, A. R. Blaustein, and P. J. Bartlein. 2010b. Projected climate-induced faunal change in the Western Hemisphere. Ecology 90:588-597. Leatherman, D. A., I. Aguayo, and T. M. Mehall. 2009a. Mountain pine beetle. Available at http://www.ext.colostate.edu/pubs/insect/05528.html. Colorado State University, Fort Collins, Colorado, USA.

Lawler, J. J., T. H. Tear, C. Pyke, M. R. Shaw, P. Gonzalez, P. Kareiva, L. Hansen, L. Hannah, K. Klausmeyer, A. Aldous, C. Bienz, and S. Pearsall. 2010a. Resource management in a changing and uncertain climate. Frontiers in Ecology and the Environment 8:35–43.

Leatherman, D. A., J. W. Brewer, and R. E. Stevens. 2009b. Western spruce budworms. Available at http://www.ext.colostate.edu/pubs/insect/05543.html. Colorado State University, Fort Collins, Colorado, USA.

Lenarz, M. S., M. E. Nelson, M. W. Schrage, and A. J. Edwards. 2009. Temperature Mediated Moose Survival in Northeastern Minnesota. Journal of Wildlife Management 73:503–510.

Lenihan, J. M., D. Bachelet, R. P. Neilson, and R. Drapek. 2008. Simulated response of conterminous United States ecosystems to climate change at different levels of fire suppression, CO_2 emission rate, and growth response to CO_2. Global and Planetary Change 64:16–25.

Lesica, P., and B. McCune. 2004. Decline of arctic-alpine plants at the southern margin of their range following a decade of climatic warming. Journal of Vegetation Science 15:679–690.

Littell, J. S., D. McKenzie, D. L. Peterson, and A. L. Westerling. 2009. Climate and wildfire area burned in western U. S. ecoprovinces, 1916–2003. Ecological Applications 19:1003–1021.

Lindroth, R. L., K. K. Kinney, and C. L. Platz. 1993. Responses of deciduous trees to elevated atmospheric CO_2: Productivity, phytochemistry, and insect performance. Ecology 74:763–777.

Little, E. L. 1971. Atlas of United States trees. Volume 1, Conifers and important hardwoods. USDA Forest Service, Miscellaneous Publications 1146. Washington , D. C., USA.

Loarie, S. R., P. B. Duffy, H. Hamilton, G. P. Asner, C. B. Field, and D. D. Ackerly. 2009. The velocity of climate change. Nature 462:1052-1055.

Logan, J. A., J. Regniere, and J. A. Powell. 2003. Assessing the impacts of global warming on forest pest dynamics. Frontiers in Ecology and the Environment 1:130–137.

Loreau, M., S. Naeem, P. Inchausti, J. Bengtsson, J. P. Grime, A. Hector, D. U. Hooper, M. A. Huston, D. Raffaelli, B. Schmid, D. Tilman, and D. A. Wardle. 2001. Ecology—Biodiversity and ecosystem functioning: Current knowledge and future challenges. Science 294:804–808.

Lowe, P. N., W. K. Lauenroth, and I. C. Burke. 2003. Effects of nitrogen availability on competition between *Bromus tectorum* and *Bouteloua gracilis*. Plant Ecology 167:247–254.

Luckman, B., and T. Kavanagh. 2000. Impact of climate fluctuations on mountain environments in the Canadian Rockies. AMBIO: A Journal of the Human Environment 29:371–380.

MacArthur, R. H., and L. C. Wang. 1974. Behavioral thermoregulation in the pika *Ochotona princeps*: A field study using radiotelemetry. Canadian Journal of Zoology 52:353–358.

MacArthur, R. H., and E. O. Wilson. 1967. The theory of island biogeography. Princeton University Press, Princeton, New Jersey, USA.

Mack, R. N. 1986. Alien plant invasion into the Intermountain West: A case history. Pages 192–213 *in* H. A. Mooney and J. Drake, editors. Ecology of biological invasions of North America and Hawaii. Springer-Verlag, New York, New York, USA.

Malanson, G. P., D. R. Butler, and D. B. Fagre. 2007a. Alpine ecosystem dynamics and change: A view from the heights. Pages 85–101 *in* T. Prato and D. B. Fagre, editors. Sustaining Rocky Mountain landscapes: Science, policy, and management of the Crown of the Continent Ecosystem. Resources for the Future, Washington, D.C., USA.

Malanson, G. P., D. R. Butler, D. B. Fagre, S. J. Walsh, D. F. Tomback, L. D. Daniels, L. M. Resler, W. K. Smith, D. J. Weiss, D. L. Peterson, A. G. Bunn, C. A. Hiemstra, D. Liptzin, P. S. Bourgeron, Z. Shen, and C. I. Millar. 2007b. Alpine treeline of Western North America: Linking organism-to-landscape dynamics. Physical Geography 28:378–396.

Mattson, D. J., and D. P. Reinhart. 1997. Excavation of red squirrel middens by grizzly bears in the whitebark pine zone. Journal of Applied Ecology 34:926–940.

Mawdsley, J. R., R. O'Malley, and D. S. Ojima. 2009. A review of climate-change adaptation strategies for wildlife management and biodiversity conservation. Conservation Biology 23:1080–1089.

McCarty, J. P. 2001. Ecological consequences of recent climate change. Conservation Biology 15:320–331.

McKenzie, D., Z. Gedalof, D. L. Peterson, and P. Mote. 2004. Climatic change, wildfire, and conservation. Conservation Biology 18:890–902.

McLaughlin, J. F., J. J. Hellmann, C. L. Boggs, and P. R. Ehrlich. 2002. Climate change hastens population extinctions. Proceedings of the National Academy of Sciences of the United States of America 99:6070–6074.

McMenamin, S. K., E. A. Hadly, and C. K. Wright. 2008. Climatic change and wetland desiccation cause amphibian decline in Yellowstone National Park. Proceedings of the National Academy of Sciences of the United States of America 105:16988–16993.

McWethy, D. (in press). Observed and projected trends in climate and associated ecosystem effects: A synthesis of the best available science. NPS Natural Resources Report, Fort Collins, CO.

Meko, D. M., C. A. Woodhouse, C. A. Baisan, T. Knight, J. J. Lukas, M. K. Hughes, and M. W. Salzer. 2007. Medieval drought in the upper Colorado River Basin. Geophysical Research Letters 34.

Meyer, J. L., and R. T. Edwards. 1990. Ecosystem metabolism and turnover of organic carbon along a Blackwater River continuum. Ecology 71:668–677.

Millar, C. I., N. L. Stephenson, and S. L. Stephens. 2007. Climate change and forests of the future: Managing in the face of uncertainty. Ecological Applications 17:2145–2151.

Millar, C. I., and R. Westfall. 2010. Distribution and climatic relationships of the American pika (*Ochotona princeps*) in the Sierra Nevada and Western Great Basin, USA; Periglacial landforms as refugia in warming climates. Arctic, Antarctic, and Alpine Research 42:76–88.

Miller, R. F., J. D. Bates, T. J. Svejcar, F. Pierson, and L. Eddleman. 2005. Biology, ecology, and management of western juniper. Tech. Bull. 152. Oregon State University, Agricultural Experiment Station, Corvallis, Oregon, USA.

Miller, R. F., and R. J. Tausch. 2001. The role of fire in juniper and pinyon woodlands: A descriptive analysis. Pages 15–30 in K.E.M. Galley and T.P. Wilson, editors. Proceedings of the invasive species workshop: The role of fire in the control and spread of invasive species. Fire conference 2000: First National Congress on Fire Ecology, Prevention, and Management. Miscellaneous publication No. 11, Tall Timbers Research Station Tallahassee, Florida, USA.

Mitsch, W. J., and J. G. Gosselink. 2007. Wetlands. 4th edition. Wiley & Sons, Inc., Hoboken, New Jersey, USA.

Mitton, J. B., and M. C. Grant. 1996. Genetic variation and the natural history of quaking aspen. BioScience 46:25–31.

Mohseni, O., H. G. Stefan, and J. G. Eaton. 2003. Global warming and potential changes in fish habitat in US Streams. Climatic Change 59:389–409.

Monaco, T. A., D. A. Johnson, J. M. Norton, T. A. Jones, K. J. Connors, J. B. Norton, and M. B. Redinbaugh. 2003. Contrasting responses of intermountain west grasses to soil nitrogen. Journal of Range Management 56:282–290.

Morgan, P., E. K. Heyerdahl, and C. E. Gibson. 2008. Multi-season climate synchronized forest fires throughout the 20th century, Northern Rockies, USA. Ecology 89:717-728.

Morgan, J. A., D. R. Lecain, A. R. Mosier, and D. G. Milchunas. 2001. Elevated CO_2 enhances water relations and productivity and affects gas exchange in C3 and C4 grasses of the Colorado shortgrass steppe. Global Change Biology 7:451–466.

Morgan, J. A., D. G. Milchunas, D. R. LeCain, M. West, and A. R. Mosier. 2007. Carbon dioxide enrichment alters plant community structure and accelerates shrub growth in the shortgrass steppe. Proceedings of the National Academy of Sciences of the United States of America 104:14724–14729.

Morgan, J. A., A. R. Mosier, D. G. Milchunas, D. R. LeCain, J. A. Nelson, and W. J. Parton. 2004. CO_2 enhances productivity, alters species composition, and reduces digestibility of shortgrass steppe vegetation. Ecological Applications 14:208–219.

Moritz, C., J. L. Patton, C. J. Conroy, J. L. Parra, G. C. White, and S. R. Beissinger. 2008. Impact of a century of climate change on small-mammal communities in Yosemite National Park, USA. Science 322:261–264.

Morrison, J. Climate change in the Kootenai, *in prep.*

Morrison, J., M. C. Quick, and M. G. G. Foreman. 2002. Climate change in the Fraser River watershed: Flow and temperature projections. Journal of Hydrology 263:230–244.

Morrison, S. F., and D. S. Hik. 2007. Demographic analysis of a declining pika *Ochotona collaris* population: Linking survival to broad-scale climate patterns via spring snowmelt patterns. Journal of Animal Ecology 76:899–907.

Mote, P. W. 2003. Trends in snow water equivalent in the Pacific Northwest and their climatic causes. Geophysical Research Letters 30:1601.

Mote, P. W., A. F. Hamlet, M. P. Clark, and D. P. Lettenmaier. 2005. Declining mountain snow-pack in western North America. Bulletin of the American Meteorological Society 86:39–49.

MTNHP [Montana Natural Heritage Program]. 2009. Montana animal species of concern. Montana Natural Heritage Program and Montana Fish, Wildlife, and Parks. http://fwp.mt.gov/wildthings/concern/

Muths, E., D. S. Pilliod, and L. J. Livo. 2008. Distribution and environmental limitations of an amphibian pathogen in the Rocky Mountains, USA. Biological Conservation 141:1484–1492.

National Assessment Synthesis Team. 2001. Climate change impacts on the United States: The potential consequences of climate variability and change. Report for the US Global Change Research Program, Cambridge University Press, Cambridge, UK.

Neff, J. C., A. P. Ballantyne, G. L. Farmer, N. M. Mahowald, J. L. Conroy, C. C. Landry, J. T. Overpeck, T. H. Painter, C. R. Lawrence, and R. L. Reynolds. 2008. Increasing eolian dust deposition in the western United States linked to human activity. Nature Geoscience 1:189–195.

Negron, J. F., B. J. Bentz, C. J. Fettig, N. Gillette, E. M. Hansen, J. L. Hays, R. G. Kelsey, J. E. Lundquist, A. M. Lynch, R. A. Progar, and S. J. Seybold. 2008. USDA Forest Service bark beetle research in the western United States: Looking toward the future. Journal of Forestry 106:325–331.

Neilson, R. P., L. F. Pitelka, A. M. Solomon, R. A. N. Nathan, G. F. Midgley, J. M. V. Fragoso, H. Lischke, and K. E. N. Thompson. 2005. Forecasting regional to global plant migration in response to climate change. BioScience 55:749–759.

Neuenschwander, L. F., J. W. Byler, A. E. Harvey, G. I. McDonald, D. S. Ortiz, H. L. Osborne, G. C. Snyder, and A. C. Zack. 1999. White pine in the American west: A vanishing species—Can we save it? General Technical Report RMRS-GTR-35. USDA Forest Service, Rocky Mountain Research Station, Fort Collins, Colorado, USA.

NICC [National Interagency Coordination Center]. 2010. Fire Information—Wildland Fire Statistics. Available at http://www.nifc.gov/fire_info/ytd_state_2009.htm.

NISIC [National Invasive Species Information Center]. 2010. What is an invasive species? Available at http://www.invasivespeciesinfo.gov/whatis.shtml.

Niven, D. K., G. S. Butcher, G. T. Bancroft, W. B. Monahan, and G. Langham. 2009. Birds and climate change: Ecological disruption in motion. http://www.audubon.org/news/pressroom/bacc/pdfs/Birds%20and%20Climate%20Report.pdf. Audubon Society, New York, New York, USA.

Noss, RF, E.T. LaRoe, J.M. Scott. 1995. Endangered ecosystems of the United States: A preliminary assessment of loss and degradation. Biological Report. US Fish and Wildlife Service.

NPS [National Park Service]. 2008. Yellowstone Superintendent's Report. Yellowstone National Park, Wyoming, USA.

NWHC [National Wildlife Health Center, USGS]. 2010. White-nose syndrome. Available at http://www.nwhc.usgs.gov/disease_information/white-nose_syndrome/.

NWSR [National Wild and Scenic Rivers]. 2010. Designated wild and scenic rivers. Available at http://www.rivers.gov/wildriverslist.html..

Ogden, N. H., A. Maarouf, I. K. Barker, M. Bigras-Poulin, L. R. Lindsay, M. G. Morshed, C. J. O'Callaghan, F. Ramay, D. Waltner-Toews, and D. F. Charron. 2006. Climate change and the potential for range expansion of the Lyme disease vector *Ixodes scapularis* in Canada. International Journal for Parasitology 36:63–70.

Opdam, P., and D. Wascher. 2004. Climate change meets habitat fragmentation: Linking landscape and biogeographical scale levels in research and conservation. Biological Conservation 117:285–297.

OTA [Office of Technology Assessment]. 1993. Wetlands. Preparing for an uncertain climate, Vol. II OTA-O-568. US Congress, Washington, D.C., USA.

Parmesan, C. 1996. Climate and species range. Nature 382:765–766.

Parmesan, C. 2006. Ecological and evolutionary responses to recent climate change. Annual Review of Ecology, Evolution, and Systematics 37:637–669.

Parmesan, C., and G. Yohe. 2003. A globally coherent fingerprint of climate change impacts across natural systems. Nature 421:37–42.

Parton, W. J., M. P. Gutmann, S. A. Williams, M. Easter, and D. Ojima. 2005. Ecological impact of historical land-use patterns in the great plains: A methodological assessment. Ecological Applications 15:1915-1928.

Parton, W. J., D. S. Ojima, and D. S. Schimel. 1994. Environmental change in grasslands: Assessment using models. Climatic Change 28:111–141

Patla, D. A., C. R. Peterson, and P. S. Corn. 2009. Amphibian decline in Yellowstone National Park. Proceedings of the National Academy of Sciences 106:E22–E22.

Patten, D. T. 1998. Riparian ecosystems of semi-arid North America: Diversity and human impacts. Wetlands 18:498–512.

Patz, J. A., T. K. Graczyk, N. Geller, and A. Y. Vittor. 2000. Effects of environmental change on emerging parasitic diseases. International Journal for Parasitology 30:1395–1405.

Pauchard, A., C. Kueffer, H. Dietz, C. C. Daehler, J. Alexander, P. J. Edwards, J. R. Arevalo, L. A. Cavieres, A. Guisan, S. Haider, G. Jakobs, K. McDougall, C. I. Millar, B. J. Naylor, C. G. Parks, L. J. Rew, and T. Seipel. 2009. Ain't no mountain high enough: Plant invasions reaching new elevations. Frontiers in Ecology and the Environment 7:479–486.

Pederson, G. T., D. B. Fagre, S. T. Gray, and L. J. Graumlich. 2004. Decadal-scale climate drivers for glacial dynamics in Glacier National Park, Montana, USA. Geophysical Research Letters 31:L12203.

Pederson, G. T., L. J. Graumlich, D. B. Fagre, T. Kipfer, and C. C. Muhlfeld. 2010. A century of climate and ecosystem change in western Montana: What do temperature trends portend? Climatic Change 98:133–154.

Pederson, G., C. Whitlock, E. Watson, B. Luckman, and L. J. Graumlich. 2007. Paleoperspectives on climate and ecosystem change. Pages 151–170 *in* T. Prato and D. B. Fagre, editors. Sustaining Rocky Mountain landscapes: Science, policy, and management of the Crown of the Continent Ecosystem. Resources for the Future, Washington, D.C., USA.

Perfors, T., J. Harte, and S. E. Alter. 2003. Enhanced growth of sagebrush (*Artemisia tridentata*) in response to manipulated ecosystem warming. Global Change Biology 9:736–742.

Perry, D. A. 1994. Forest ecosystems. Johns Hopkins University Press, Baltimore, Maryland, USA.

Peterson, D. L., and D. McKenzie. 2008. Wildland fire and climate change. Available at http://www.fs.fed.us/ccrc/topics/wildland-fire.shtml. USDA Forest Service, Climate Change Resource Center.

Peterson, D. P., K. D. Fausch, J. Watmough, and R. A. Cunjak. 2008. When eradication is not an option: Modeling strategies for electrofishing suppression of nonnative brook trout to foster persistence of sympatric native cutthroat trout in small streams. North American Journal of Fisheries Management 28:1847–1867.

Petersen, J. H., and J. F. Kitchell. 2001. Climate regimes and water temperature changes in the Columbia River: Bioenergetic implications for predators of juvenile salmon. Canadian Journal of Fisheries and Aquatic Sciences 58:1831–1841.

Picton, H. D. 1984. Climate and the prediction of reproduction of three ungulate species. Journal of Applied Ecology 21:869–879.

Pitelka, L. F. 1997. Plant migration and climate change. American Scientist 85:464.

Poff, N. L., M. M. Brinson, and J. W. Day. 2002. Aquatic ecosystems and global climate change. Pew Center on Global Climate Change, Arlington, Virginia, USA.

Poore, R. E., C. A. Lamanna, J. J. Ebersole, and B. J. Enquist. 2009. Controls on radial growth of mountain big sagebrush and implications for climatic change. Western North American Naturalist 69:556–562.

Post, E., and N. C. Stenseth. 1999. Climatic variability, plant phenology, and northern ungulates. Ecology 80:1322–1339.

Pounds, J. A., M. R. Bustamante, L. A. Coloma, J. A. Consuegra, M. P. L. Fogden, P. N. Foster, E. La Marca, K. L. Masters, A. Merino-Viteri, R. Puschendorf, S. R. Ron, G. A. Sanchez-Azofeifa, C. J. Still, and B. E. Young. 2006. Widespread amphibian extinctions from epidemic disease driven by global warming. Nature 439:161–167.

Pounds, J. A., and M. L. Crump. 1994. Amphibian declines and climate disturbance: The case of the golden toad and the harlequin frog. Conservation Biology 8:72–85.

Pounds, J. A., M. P. Fogden, and J. H. Campbell. 1999. Biological response to climate change on a tropical mountain. Nature 398:611–615.

Prevey, J. S., M. J. Germino, N. J. Huntly, and R. S. Inouye. 2010. Exotic plants increase and native plants decrease with loss of foundation species in sagebrush steppe. Plant Ecology 207:39–51.

Price, J. T., and T. L. Root. 2005. Potential impacts of climate change on neotropical migrants: Management implications. Pages 1123-1128 in C.J. Ralph and T.D. Rich, editors. Bird conservation implementation and integration in the Americas: Proceedings of the Third International Partners in Flight Conference, Pacific Southwest Research Station, PSW-GTR-191.

Raffa, K. F., B. H. Aukema, B. J. Bentz, C. A.L., J. A. Hicke, M. G. Turner, and W. H. Romme. 2008. Cross-scale drivers of natural disturbances prone to anthropogenic amplification: Dynamics of biome-wide bark beetle eruptions. BioScience 58:501–517.

Rahel, F. J., and J. D. Olden. 2008. Assessing the effects of climate change on aquatic invasive species. Conservation Biology 22:521–533.

Ray, A. J., J. J. Barsugli, and K. B. Averyt. 2008. Climate change in Colorado: A synthesis to support water resources management and adaptation. A report by the Western Water Assessment for the Colorado Water Conservation Board. CU–NOAA Western Water Assessment, Boulder, Colorado, USA.

Ray, A. J., J. J. Barsugli, K. Wolter, and J. K. Eischeid. 2010. Rapid-response climate assessment to support the FWS status review of the American pika. NOAA Earth Systems Research Laboratory, Boulder, Colorado, USA.

Rehfeldt, G. E., D. E. Ferguson, and N. L. Crookston. 2009. Aspen, climate, and sudden decline in western USA. Forest Ecology and Management 258:2353–2364.

Rehfeldt, G., W. Wykoff, and C. Ying. 2001. Physiologic plasticity, evolution, and impacts of a changing climate on *Pinus Contorta*. Climatic Change 50:355–376.

Reinhart, D. P., M. A. Haroldson, D. J. Mattson, and K. A. Gunther. 2001. Effects of exotic species on Yellowstone's grizzly bears. Western North American Naturalist 61:277–288.

Reisen, W. K., Y. Fang, and V. M. Martinez. 2009. Effects of temperature on the transmission of West Nile virus by *Culex tarsalis* (Diptera: Culicidae). Journal of Medical Entomology 43:309–317.

Rice, A. V., and D. W. Langor. 2009. Mountain pine beetle-associated blue-stain fungi in lodgepole–jack pine hybrids near Grande Prairie, Alberta (Canada). Forest Pathology 39:323–334.

Rieman, B. E., D. Isaak, S. Adams, D. Horan, D. Nagel, C. Luce, and D. Myers. 2007. Anticipated climate warming effects on bull trout habitats and populations across the interior Columbia River basin. Transactions of the American Fisheries Society 136:1552–1565.

Ripple, W. J., and R. L. Beschta. 2004. Wolves and the ecology of fear: Can predation risk structure ecosystems? BioScience 54:755–766.

Rodhouse, T. J., E.A. Beever, L.K. Garrett, K.M. Irvine, M. Munts, C. Ray, and M. R. Shardlow. 2010. Distribution of American pikas in a low-elevation lava landscape: Conservation implications from the range periphery. Journal of Mammalogy 91(5): *in press.*

Roland, J., and S. F. Matter. 2007. Encroaching forests decouple alpine butterfly population dynamics. Proceedings of the National Academy of Sciences of the United States of America 104:13702–13704.

Romme, W. H., J. Clement, J. Hicke, D. Kulakowski, L. H. MacDonald, T. Schoennagel, and T. Veblen. 2006. Recent forest insect outbreaks and fire risk in Colorado forests: A brief synthesis of relevant research. Colorado Forest Restoration Institute, Fort Collins, Colorado, USA.

Romme, W. H., D. H. Knight, and J. B. Yavitt. 1986. Mountain pine beetle outbreaks in the Rocky Mountains: Regulators of primary productivity? The American Naturalist 127:484–494.

Romme, W. H., M. G. Turner, G. A. Tuskan, and R. A. Reed. 2005. Establishment, persistence, and growth of aspen (*Populus tremuloides*) seedlings in Yellowstone National Park. Ecology 86:404–418.

Root, T. L., J. T. Price, K. R. Hall, S. H. Schneider, C. Rosenzweig, and J. A. Pounds. 2003. Fingerprints of global warming on wild animals and plants. Nature 421:57–60.

Rowland, M. M., L. H. Suring, R. J. Tausch, S. Geer, and M. J. Wisdom. 2008. Characteristics of western juniper encroachment into sagebrush communities in central Oregon. USDA Forest Service Forestry and Range Sciences Laboratory, La Grande, Oregon, USA.

Rowland, M. M., M. J. Wisdom, L. H. Suring, and C. W. Meinke. 2006. Greater sage-grouse as an umbrella species for sagebrush-associated vertebrates. Biological Conservation 129:323–335.

Running, S. W. 2009. Impacts of climate change on forests of the northern Rocky Mountains. Available at http://www.bipartisanpolicy.org/library/research/impacts-climate-change-forests-northern-rocky-mountains.

Rustad, L. E., J. L. Campbell, G. M. Marion, R. J. Norby, M. J. Mitchell, A. E. Hartley, J. H. C. Cornelissen, J. Gurevitch, and N. Gcte. 2001. A meta-analysis of the response of soil respiration, net nitrogen mineralization, and aboveground plant growth to experimental ecosystem warming. Oecologia 126:543–562.

Ryan, M. G., S. R. Archer, R. Birdsey, C. Dahm, L. Heath, J. Hicke, D. Hollinger, T. Huxman, G. Okin, R. Oren, J. Randerson, and Schlesinger, W. H. 2008. Land resources: Forests and Arid Lands. Pages 75–120 in P. Backlund, A. Janetos, D. Schimel, M. Walsh, editors. The effects of climate change on agriculture, land resources, water resources, and biodiversity in the United States. A Report by the US Climate Change Science Program and the Subcommittee on Global Change Research. US Department of Agriculture, Washington, D.C., USA.

Sage, R., and D. Kubien. 2003. Quo vadis C4? An ecophysiological perspective on global change and the future of C4 plants. Photosynthesis Research 77:209–225.

Salzer, M. W., M. K. Hughes, A. G. Bunn, and K. F. Kipfmueller. 2009. Recent unprecedented tree-ring growth in bristlecone pine at the highest elevations and possible causes. Proceedings of the National Academy of Sciences of the United States of America 106:20348–20353.

Sawyer, H., F. Lindzey, and D. McWhirter. 2005. Mule deer and pronghorn migration in western Wyoming. Wildlife Society Bulletin 33:1266–1273.

SCBD [Secretariat of the Convention on Biological Diversity]. 2003. Interlinkages between biological diversity and climate change. Advice on the integration of biodiversity considerations into the implementation of the United Nations Framework Convention on Climate Change and its Kyoto protocol., Montreal, Canada.

Schade, C. B., and S. A. Bonar. 2005. Distribution and abundance of nonnative fishes in streams of the western United States. North American Journal of Fisheries Management 25:1386–1394.

Schmitz, O. J., E. Post, C. E. Burns, and K. M. Johnston. 2003. Ecosystem responses to global climate change: Moving beyond color mapping. BioScience 53:1199-1205.

Schoennagel, T., T. T. Veblen, W. H. Romme, J. S. Sibold, and E. R. Cook. 2005. ENSO and PDO variability affect drought-induced fire occurance in Rocky Mountain subalpine forests. Ecological Applications 15:2000–2014.

Schrag, A. M., A. G. Bunn, and L. J. Graumlich. 2008. Influence of bioclimatic variables on treeline conifer distribution in the Greater Yellowstone Ecosystem: Implications for species of conservation concern. Journal of Biogeography 35:698–710.

Schreiber, R. W., and E.A. Schreiber 1984. Central pacific seabirds and the El Nino-Southern Oscillation: 1982–1983 perspectives. Science 225:713–716.

Schwartz, C. C., M. A. Haroldson, G. C. White, R. B. Harris, S. Cherry, K. A. Keating, D. Moody, and C. Servheen. 2006. Temporal, spatial, and environmental influences on the demographics of grizzly bears in the Greater Yellowstone Ecosystem. Wildlife Monographs:1–68.

Scott, M. L., J. M. Friedman, and G. T. Auble. 1996. Fluvial process and the establishment of bottomland trees. Geomorphology 14:327-339.

Scott, M. L., P. B. Shafroth, and G. T. Auble. 1999. Responses of riparian cottonwoods to alluvial water table declines. Environmental Management 23:347-358.

Seastedt, T. 2002. Base camps of the Rockies: The intermountain grasslands. Pages 219–236 *in* J. S. Baron, editor. Rocky Mountain futures: An ecological perspective. Island Press, Washington, D.C., USA.

Seastedt, T. R., W. D. Bowman, T. N. Caine, D. McKnight, A. Townsend, and M. W. Williams. 2004. The landscape continuum: A model for high-elevation ecosystems. BioScience 54:111–121.

Sekercioglu, C. H., S. H. Schneider, J. P. Fay, and S. R. Loarie. 2008. Climate change, elevational range shifts, and bird extinctions. Conservation Biology 22:140–150.

Shaw, J. D., B. E. Steed, and L. T. DeBlander. 2005. Forest inventory and analysis (FIA) annual inventory answers the question: What is happening to pinyon-juniper woodlands? Journal of Forestry 103:280–285.

Sheppard, P. R., A. C. Comrie, G. D. Packin, K. Angersbach, and M. K. Hughes. 2002. The climate of the US Southwest. Climate Research 21:219-238.

Shepperd, W. D., D. L. Bartos, and S. A. Mata. 2001a. Above- and below-ground effects of aspen clonal regeneration and succession to conifers. Canadian Journal Of Forest Research-Revue Canadienne De Recherche Forestiere 31:739–745.

Shepperd, W. D., D. Binkley, D. L. Bartos, T. J. Stohlgren, and L. G. Eskew. 2001b. Sustaining aspen in western landscapes, symposium proceedings, 13-15 June 2000,; Grand Junction, Colorado. Proceedings RMRS-P-18. USDA Forest Service, Rocky Mountain Research Station, Fort Collins, Colorado, USA.

Sherriff, R. L., and T. T. Veblen. 2008. Variability in fire-climate relationships in ponderosa pine forests in the Colorado front range. International Journal of Wildland Fire 17:50-59.

Shoo, L. P., S. E. Williams, and J. M. Hero. 2005. Potential decoupling of trends in distribution area and population size of species with climate change. Global Change Biology 11:1469–1476.

Sibold, J. S., and T. T. Veblen. 2006. Relationships of subalpine forest fires in the Colorado front range to interannual and multi-decadal scale climatic variation. Journal of Biogeography 33:833–842.

Sibold, J. S., T. T. Veblen and M. E. Gonzalez. 2006. Spatial and temporal variation in historic fire regimes in subalpine forests across the Colorado front range in Rocky Mountain National Park. Journal of Biogeography 32:631–647.

Smith, A. T., and M. L. Weston. 1990. *Ochotona princeps*. Mammalian Species:1–8.

Smith, S. D., R. K. Monson, and J.E. Anderson. 1997. Physiological ecology of North American desert plants. Springer-Verlag, Berlin.

Smith, S. D., T. E. Huxman, S. F. Zitzer, T. N. Charlet, D. C. Housman, J. S. Coleman, L. K. Fenstermaker, J. R. Seemann, and R. S. Nowak. 2000. Elevated CO_2 increases productivity and invasive species success in an arid ecosystem. Nature 408:79–82.

Smith, W. B., J. S. Vissage, D. R. Darr, and R. M. Sheffield. 2001. Forest resources of the United States, 1997. General Technical Report NC-219. USDA Forest Service, North Central Research Station, St. Paul, Minnesota, USA.

Soule, P. T., P. A. Knapp, and H. D. Grissino-Mayer. 2004. Human agency, environmental drivers, and western juniper establishment during the late holocene. Ecological Applications 14:96–112.

Sparks, T. H., F. Bairlein, J. G. Bojarinova, O. Huppop, E. A. Lehikoinen, K. Rainio, L. V. Sokolov, and D. Walker. 2005. Examining the total arrival distribution of migratory birds. Global Change Biology 11:22–30.

Steltzer, H., C. Landry, T. H. Painter, J. Anderson, and E. Ayres. 2009. Biological consequences of earlier snowmelt from desert dust deposition in alpine landscapes. Proceedings of the National Academy of Sciences of the United States of America 106:11629–11634.

Steltzer, H., and E. Post. 2009. Seasons and life cycles. Science 324:886–887.

Stenseth, M. C., A. Mysterud, G. Ottersen, J. W. Hurrell, K.S. Chan, and M. Lima. 2002. Ecological effects of climate fluctuations. Science 297:1292–1296.

Stewart, I. T., D. R. Cayan, and M. D. Dettinger. 2005. Changes toward earlier streamflow timing across western North America. Journal of Climate 18:1136–1155.

Stewart, M. M. 1995. Climate driven population fluctuations in rain forest frogs. Journal of Herpetology 29:437-466.

Stohlgren, T. J., T. T. Veblen, K. C. Kendall, W. L. Baker, C. D. Allen, J. A. Logan, and K. C. Ryan. 2002. The heart of the Rockies: Montane and subalpine ecosystems. Pages 203–218 in J. S. Baron, editor. Rocky Mountain futures: An ecological perspective. Island Press, Washington, D.C., USA.

Strand, E. K., S. C. Bunting, R. K. Steinhorst, L. K. Garrett, and G. H. Dicus. 2009. Upper Columbia Basin Network aspen monitoring protocol. Natural Resource Report NPS/UCBN/NRR-2009/147. National Park Service, Fort Collins, Colorado, USA.

Street, F. A., and A. T. Grove. 1979. Global maps of lake-level fluctuations since 30,000 yr BP. Quaternary Research 12:83–118.

Stromberg, J. C., R. Tiller, and B. Richter. 1996. Effects of groundwater decline on riparian vegetation of semiarid regions: The San Pedro, Arizona. Ecological Applications 6:113–131.

Sturm, M., C. Racine, and K. Tape. 2001. Climate change: Increasing shrub abundance in the Arctic. Nature 411:546–547.

Swetnam, T. W., and A. M. Lynch. 1993. Multicentury, regional-scale patterns of western spruce budworm outbreaks. Ecological Monographs 63:399–424.

Tagaris, E., K.-J. Liao, K. Manomaiphiboon, J.-H. Woo, S. He, P. Amar, and A. G. Russell. 2008. Impacts of future climate change and emissions reductions on nitrogen and sulfur deposition over the United States, Geophysical Research Letters 35, L08811, doi:10.1029/2008GL033477.

Taylor, P. D., L. Fahrig, K. Henein, and G. Merriam. 1993. Connectivity is a vital element of landscape structure. Oikos 68:571-573.

TNC [The Nature Conservancy]. 2009. Montana's Northern Prairies. [Available online?] Helena,Montana, USA.

Tomback, D. F., and K. C. Kendall. 2002. Rocky road in the Rockies: Challenges to biodiversity. Pages 153–180 in J. S. Baron, editor. Rocky Mountain futures: An ecological perspective. Island Press, Washington.

Ultsch, G. R., D. F. Bradford, and J. Freda. 1999. Physiology: Coping with the environment. Pages 189–214 in R. W. McDiarmid and R. Altig, editors, Tadpoles: The biology of anuran larvae. University of Chicago Press, Chicago, Illinois, USA.

USDA [US Department of Agriculture]. 2008a. Colorado forest heath highlights 2008. Available at http://www.fs.fed.us/foresthealth/fhm/fhh/fhh_08/co_fhh_08.pdf. USDA Forest Service, Fort Collins, Colorado, USA.

USDA [US Department of Agriculture]. 2008b. Wyoming forest heath highlights 2008. Available at http://www.fs.fed.us/foresthealth/fhm/fhh/fhh_08/wy_fhh_08.pdf. USDA Forest Service, Cheyenne, Wyoming, USA.

USEPA [US Environmental Protection Agency]. 1998. National air quality and emissions trends report,1997. Office of Air Quality Planning and Standards, Washington, D.C., USA.

USEPA [US Environmental Protection Agency]. 2008a. Key elements of the Clean Air Act. Available at http://www.epa.gov/air/peg/elements.html. Washington, D. C.

USEPA [US Environmental Protection Agency]. 2008b. National air quality status and trends through 2007. Office of Air Quality Planning and Standards, Washington, D.C., USA.

USFWS [US Fish and Wildlife Service]. 2010. Endangered and threatened wildlife and plants; 12-month finding on a petition to list the American pika as threatened or endangered. 50 CFR Part 17. Available online at http://www.fws.gov/mountain-prairie/species/mammals/americanpika/02052010FRTemp.pdf

USGS [US Geological Survey]. 2010. Nonindigenous aquatic species. Available at http://nas.er.usgs.gov/taxgroup/mollusks/zebramussel/. Department of the Interior.

Van Arsdel, E. P, B. W. Geils, and P. J. Zambino. 2006. Epidemiology for hazard rating of white pine blister rust. Pages 49-61 in J. Guyon, compiler. Proceedings of the 53rd Western International Forest Disease Work Conference; 26–29 August 2005; Jackson, Wyoming. USDA Forest Service, Intermountain Region, Ogden, Utah, USA.

Van Buskirk, J. R. S. Mulvihill, and R. C. Leberman. 2010. Declining body sizes in North American birds associated with climate change. Oikos 000:001-009.

Van Mantgem, P. J., and N. L. Stephenson. 2007. Apparent climatically induced increase of tree mortality rates in a temperate forest. Ecology Letters 10:909–916.

Van Ruijven, J., and F. Berendse. 2005. Diversity–productivity relationships: Initial effects, long-term patterns, and underlying mechanisms. Proceedings of the National Academy of Sciences of the United States of America 102:695–700.

Veblen, T. T., T. Kitzberger, and J. Donnegan. 2000. Climatic and human influences on fire regims in ponderosa pine forests in the Colorado front range. Ecological Applications 10:1178–1195.

Vieira, M. 2006. Moose management plan: Data analysis unit M-2 Laramie River herd. Colorado Division of Wildlife, Fort Collins, Colorado, USA.

Vingarzan, R. 2004. A review of surface ozone background levels and trends. Atmospheric Environment 38:3431–3442.

Visser, M. E., and C. Both. 2005. Shifts in phenology due to global climate change: The need for a yardstick. Proceedings of the Royal Society of London, Series B 272:2561–2569.

Vitousek, P. M. 1992. Global environmental change: An introduction. Annual Review of Ecology and Systematics 23:1–14.

Vitousek, P. M., H. A. Mooney, J. Lubchenco, and J. M. Melillo. 1997. Human domination of Earth's ecosystems. Science 277:494–499.

Volney, W. J. A., and R. A. Fleming. 2000. Climate change and impacts of boreal forest insects. Agriculture, Ecosystems & Environment 82:283–294.

Vose, R. S., D. Wuertz, T. C. Peterson, and P. D. Jones. 2005. An intercomparison of trends in surface air temperature analyses at the global, hemispheric, and grid-box scale. Geophysical Research Letters 32.

Walker, M. D., C. H. Wahren, R. D. Hollister, G. H. R. Henry, L. E. Ahlquist, J. M. Alatalo, M. S. Bret-Harte, M. P. Calef, T. V. Callaghan, A. B. Carroll, and others. 2006. Plant community responses to experimental warming across the tundra biome. Proceedings of the National Academy of Sciences of the United States of America 103:1342–1346.

Walker, M. D., D. A. Walker, T. A. Theodose, and P. J. Webber. 2001. The vegetation: Hierarchial species-environment relationships. Pages 99–127 *in* W. D. Bowman and T. Seastedt, editors. Structure and function of an alpine ecosystem. Oxford University Press, Niwot Ridge, Colorado, USA.

Walther, G. R., S. Beißner, C. A. Burga, and P. S. White. 2005. Trends in the upward shift of alpine plants. Journal of Vegetation Science 16:541–548.

Walther, G. R., S. Beißner, C. A. Burga, and P. S. White. 2005. Trends in the upward shift of alpine plants. Journal of Vegetation Science 16:541–548.

Walther, G. R., E. Post, P. Convey, A. Menzel, C. Parmesan, T. J. C. Beebee, J. M. Fromentin, O. Hoegh-Guldberg, and F. Bairlein. 2002. Ecological responses to recent climate change. Nature 416:389–395.

Wang, G., N. Thompson Hobbs, F. J. Singer, D. S. Ojima, and B. C. Lubow. 2002. Impacts of Climate Changes on Elk Population Dynamics in Rocky Mountain National Park, Colorado, USA. Climatic Change 54:205–223.

Wang, H., S. Schubert, M. Suarez, J. Chen, M. Hoerling, A. Kumar, and P. Pegion. 2008. Attribution of the seasonality and regionality in climate trends over the United States during 1950–2000. Journal of Climate 22:2571–2590.

Waters, T. F. 1995. Sediment in streams: Sources, biological effects, and control. American Fisheries Society Monograph 7.

Werner, E. E., R. A. Relyea, K. L. Yurewicz, D. K. Skelly, and C. J. Davis. 2009. Comparative landscape dynamics of two anuran species: Climate-driven interaction of local and regional processes. Ecological Monographs 79:503–521.

West, N. E., and J. A. Young. 2000. Intermountain valleys and lower mountain slopes. Pages 255–284 in M. G. Barbour and W. D. Billings, editors. North American terrestrial vegetation. Cambridge University Press, Cambridge, UK.

Westerling, A., and B. Bryant. 2008. Climate change and wildfire in California. Climatic Change 87:231–249.

Westerling, A. L., H. G. Hidalgo, D. R. Cayan, and T. W. Swetnam. 2006. Warming and earlier spring increase western US forest wildfire activity. Science 313:940–943.

WGFD [Wyoming Game and Fish Department]. 2005. Wyoming's species of greatest conservation need. http://gf.state.wy.us/wildlife/CompConvStrategy/CWCSSpeciesList050505.pdf. http://gf.state.wy.us/wildlife/CompConvStrategy/CWCSSpeciesList050505.pdf

Whitlock, C., and P. J. Bartlein. 1993. Spatial variations of holocene climatic change in the Yellowstone region. Quaternary research 39:231–238.

Whitlock, C., J. Marlon, C. Briles, A. Brunelle, C. Long, and P. Bartlein. 2008. Long-term relations among fire, fuel, and climate in the northwestern US based on lake-sediment studies. International Journal of Wildland Fire 17:72–83.

Whitlock, C., M. A. Reasoner, and C. H. Key. 2002. Paleoenvironmental history of the rocky mountain region during the past 20,000 years. Pages 41–57 *in* J. S. Baron, editor. Rocky Mountain futures: An ecological perspective. Island Press, Washington, D.C., USA.

Whitlock, C., S. L. Shafer, and J. Marlon. 2003. The role of climate and vegetation change in shaping past and future fire regimes in the northwestern US and the implications for ecosystem management. Forest Ecology and Management 178:5–21.

Wickham, J. D., T. G. Wade, K. B. Jones, K. H. Riitters, and R. V. O'Neill. 1995. Diversity of ecological communities of the United States. Vegetatio 119:91–100.

Williams, J. E., N. G. Gillespie, H. M. Nelville, and W. T. Colyer. 2007. Healing troubled waters: Preparing trout and salmon habitat for a changing climate. Trout Unlimited, Arlington, Virginia, USA.

Williams, J. E., A. L. Haak, H. M. Neville, and W. T. Colyer. 2009. Potential consequences of climate change to persistence of cutthroat trout populations. North American Journal of Fisheries Management 29:533–548.

Williams, M. W., and N. Caine. 2001. Hydrology and hydrochemistry. Pages 75–96 *in* W. D. Bowman and T. Seastedt, editors. Structure and function of an alpine ecosystem. Oxford University Press, Niwot Ridge, Colorado, USA.

Williams, M. W., and K. A. Tonnessen. 2000. Critical loads for inorganic nitrogen deposition in the Colorado front range, USA. Ecological Applications 10:1648–1665.

Williamson, M., and A. Fitter. 1996. The varying success of invaders. Ecology 77:1661–1666.

Winder, M., and D. E. Schindler. 2004. Climatic effects on the phenology of lake processes. Global Change Biology 10:1844–1856.

Winkler, D. W., P. O. Dunn, and C. E. McCulloch. 2002. Predicting the effects of climate change on avian life-histories. Proceedings of the National Academy of Science of the United States 99:13,595–13,599.

Winter, T. C. 2000. The vulnerability of wetlands to climate change: A hydrologic landscape perspective. Journal of the American Water Resources Association 36:305–311.

Wormworth, J., and K. Mallon. 2008. Bird species and climate change. The global status report: A synthesis of current scientific understanding of anthropogenic climate change impacts on global bird species now and projected future effects. Climate Risk Pty Limited, Fairlight, NSW.

Worrall, J. J., R. A. Mask, T. Eager, L. Egeland, and W. D. Shepperd. 2008. Sudden aspen decline in southwest Colorado. Phytopathology 98:S173–S173.

WSF [Wild Sheep Foundation]. 2010. Bighorn sheep continue to succumb to pneumonia. Available at http://www.wildsheepfoundation.org/Page.php/News/131. Cody, Wyoming, USA.

Young, P. J., A. Arneth, G. Schurgers, G. Zeng, and J. A. Pyle. 2009. The CO_2 inhibition of terrestrial isoprene emission significantly affects future ozone projections. Atmospheric Chemistry and Physics 9:2793–2803.

Zedler, J. B., and S. Kercher. 2005. Wetland resources: Status, trends, ecosystem services, and restorability. Annual Review of Environment and Resources 30:39–74.

Zier, J. L., and W. L. Baker. 2006. A century of vegetation change in the San Juan Mountains, Colorado: An analysis using repeat photography. Forest Ecology and Management 228:251–262.

The Department of the Interior protects and manages the nation's natural resources and cultural heritage; provides scientific and other information about those resources; and honors its special responsibilities to American Indians, Alaska Natives, and affiliated Island Communities.

NPS 960/104295, June 2010